The Ideals
Country
TREASURY

In the name of the Bee—
And of the Butterfly—
And of the Breeze—
EMILY DICKINSON

The Ideals
Country
TREASURY

Julie K. Hogan, Editor

IDEALS PUBLICATIONS INCORPORATED
NASHVILLE, TENNESSEE

ISBN 0-8249-4177-2

Published by Ideals Publications Incorporated
535 Metroplex Drive, Suite 250
Nashville, TN 37211

Printed and bound in the USA by RR Donnelley & Sons, Roanoke, VA.
Color Film Separations by Precision Color Graphics, New Berlin, Wisconsin.

Library of Congress Cataloging-in-Publication Number: 99-34940

First Edition
10 8 6 4 2 1 3 5 7 9

Research Assistant to the Editor, Mary P. Dunn

Publisher, Patricia A. Pingry
Book Designer, Eve DeGrie
Copy Editor, Christine Landry
Permissions, Elizabeth Kea

ADDITIONAL PHOTOGRAPHS:

Cover Photograph: Small cattle farm in Tennessee. Photo copyright Larry LeFever, Grant Heilman Photography, Inc. (W2-773D). Pages 6-7: Queen Anne's Lace growing along Middlebury River outside of Middlebury, Vermont. Photo copyright William H. Johnson, Johnson's Photography (54675-00111). Pages 30-31: A lush, green meadow along Beech Creek in Grant County, Oregon. Photo copyright Steve Terrill (OR-7-7-426). Pages 52-53: Historic Antelope Community Church, built in 1897, in Wasco County, Oregon. Photo copyright Steve Terrill (OR-7-5-1336). Pages 72-73: Sunset over Amish farms in Lancaster County, Pennsylvania. Photo copyright William H. Johnson, Johnson's Photography (43989-00101). Pages 90-91: A flock of sheep grazing in a field in Linn County, Oregon. Photo copyright Steve Terrill (OR-6-5-722). Pages 108-109: Round haybales on frosty morning in Whitfield, New Hampshire. Photo copyright by William H. Johnson, Johnson's Photography (23076-2107). Pages 130-131: Sunset over a wheatfield and chamomile in the Adirondacks of New York. Photo copyright William H. Johnson, Johnson's Photography (23389-00106).

ACKNOWLEDGMENTS

Ideals Publications Incorporated has made every effort to trace the ownership of all copyrighted material. Thanks are due to the following authors, publishers, and agents for permission to use the material indicated: APPS, JERRY. "Box Socials." From ONE-ROOM COUNTRY SCHOOLS: HISTORY AND RECOLLECTIONS FROM WISCONSIN by Jerry Apps; published by Amherst Press, a division of Palmer Publications, Inc., 318 North Main, Amherst, WI 54406; 715-824-3214. BORLAND, HAL. Excerpt from "Summer" from THIS HILL, THIS VALLEY. Reprinted by permission of Frances Collin, Literary Agent. Copyright © 1957 by Hal Borland; copyright © renewed 1985 by Barbara Dodge Borland. CHILDS, SUSAN. "Ice Cream Supper." Copyright © 1998 Southern Living, Inc. Reprinted with permission. DICKINSON, EMILY. Excerpt from "The Gentian Weaves Her Fringes" and "These are the days . . . ." Reprinted by permission of the publishers and the Trustees of Amherst College from THE POEMS OF EMILY DICKINSON, Thomas H. Johnson, ed., Cambridge, Mass.; The Belknap Press of Harvard University Press, Copyright © 1951, 1955, 1979, 1983 by the President and Fellows of Harvard College. ELLIS, MEL. "Fables and Flowers." From THE LAND, ALWAYS THE LAND by Mel Ellis. Reprinted by permission of The Cabin Bookshelf. Copyright © 1997 by The Cabin Bookshelf. FROST, ROBERT. "The Pasture" and "Putting in the Seed." From THE POETRY OF ROBERT FROST, edited by Edward Connery Lathem, Copyright 1944 by Robert Frost. Copyright © 1916, copyright © 1969 by Henry Holt and Company, LLC. Reprinted by permission of Henry Holt & Co., LLC. HALE, JUDSON SR. "Exactly What, Why, and When is Indian Summer?" from THE BEST OF THE OLD FARMER'S ALMANAC by Judson Hale, Sr. HETH, EDWARD HARRIS. "Church Supper Fare" from THE COUNTRY KITCHEN COOKBOOK. Reprinted by permission of Sternig and Byrne Literary Agency. HEYNEN, JIM. "My Father, Still a Farmer" from A SUITABLE CHURCH © by Jim Heynen. Reprinted by permission of Copper Canyon Press, Post Office Box 271, Port Townsend, WA 98368. HOLMES, MARJORIE. "Carry Me Back to the Farm" from YOU AND I AND YESTERDAY. Copyright 1973, 1987 by Marjorie Holmes. Reprinted by permission of the author. JACQUES, EDNA. "The Farm Kitchen at Night" from THE GOLDEN ROAD; "The First Church," "The Picnic to the Hills," "The School," and "Surprise Parties" from UPHILL ALL THE WAY. Copyright © in Canada by Thomas Allen & Son Limited. JONES, EVAN. "The Country Store." Copyright 1976 by Evan Jones. This usage granted by permission. KUMIN, MAXINE. "The Country Kitchen" from IN DEEP, COUNTRY ESSAYS by Maxine Kumin. Copyright 1987 by Maxine Kumin. Reprinted by permission of W. W. Norton & Company. LEOPOLD, ALDO. "The Green Pasture." From A SAND COUNTY ALMANAC: AND SKETCHES HERE AND THERE by Aldo Leopold. Copyright 1949, 1977 by Oxford University Press, Inc. Used by permission of Oxford University Press, Inc. LOGAN, BEN. "The Garden" and "Short Days and Yellow Lamplight" from THE LAND REMEMBERS. Reprinted by permission of Frances Collin, Literary Agent. Copyright © 1975 by Ben Logan. McBRIDE, MARY MARGARET. "Country Visiting." From HOW DEAR TO MY HEART by Mary Margaret McBride. Copyright 1940 by The Macillan Company. Reprinted by permission of Scribner, an imprint of Simon and Schuster, Inc. McGINNIS, R. J. "Ice Harvest" from THE GOOD OLD DAYS, copyright 1979 by R. J. McGinnis. Reprinted by permission of F & W Publications, Inc., Cincinatti, Ohio. NELSON, JOHN. "The History of Weather Vanes" from FOLK ART WEATHER VANES: AUTHENTIC AMERICAN PATTERNS FOR WOOD AND METAL by John A. Nelson. Reprinted by permission from Stackpole Books. RENNICKE, JEFF. "This Place of Summer Dreams." Copyright 1996 by Jeff Rennicke. Reprinted by permission of the author. SANDBURG, CARL. "Red and White." From HARVEST POEMS: 1910-1960, copyright © 1960, 1958 by Carl Sandburg and renewed 1988, 1986 by Margaret Sandburg, Janet Sandburg, and Helga Sandburg Crile, reprinted by permission of Harcourt, Inc. SANDERS, DORI. "Family Reunions." From DORI SANDERS' COUNTRY COOKING: RECIPES AND STORIES FROM THE FAMILY FARM STAND by Dori Sanders. Copyright © 1995 by the author. Reprinted by permission of Algonquin Books of Chapel Hill, a division of Workman Publishing. SHERROW, VICTORIA. "Huskings, Quiltings, and Barn Raisings." From HUSKINGS, QUILTINGS, AND BARN RAISINGS: WORK-PLAY PARTIES. Copyright © 1992 by Victoria Sherrow. Reprinted with permission from Walker and Company, 435 Hudson Street, New York, New York 10014; 1-800-289-2553. All rights reserved. TABER, GLADYS. "Spring" from STILLMEADOW SAMPLER by Gladys Taber. Copyright 1959 by Gladys Taber, copyright renewed 1987 by Constance Taber Colby. Reprinted by permission of Brandt & Brandt Literary Agency, Inc. Our sincere thanks to the following authors whom we were unable to locate: Margarita Cuff for "Remembering May Day"; Donald Hall for "Haying, a Horse, and a Hired Man" from A STRING TOO SHORT TO BE SAVED; Helen Ouimette for "Feather Ticks and Quilts"; Eric Sloane for "Sugaring Time"; and William and Sarah Peabody Turnbaugh for "The Mail's Here!" from MAILBOXES AND POST OFFICES OF RURAL AMERICA.

CONTENTS

Chapter One

COUNTRY FIELDS, STREAMS, AND GARDENS

Haying, a Horse, and a Hired Man

DONALD HALL

While the earth remaineth, seedtime and harvest ... and summer and winter ... shall not cease. —GENESIS 8:22

On the day I was to start my life's haying—doing what my grandfather had done for fifty years—lunch was a special occasion. Since I was not old enough to mow, I would help in the afternoons only. My Aunt Caroline was home that week, and at twelve o'clock we packed a huge laundry basket full of lunch into her car and drove to the widow's field. Near the house itself were a few fruit trees, and under one of them we spread an old quilt. There was a Thermos of coffee and a Thermos of milk, hard-boiled eggs, pork sandwiches, cheese sandwiches, an onion sandwich especially for me, pickles, cake, cookies, and a custard pie.

The brilliant orange and yellow paint brushes grew wild at the edge of the road, and beside the widow's house the lilacs were still blooming. The sky was bright, with only a few clouds, and there was a light breeze from the south. "Good day for haying," said my grandmother.

"I'll *say* it's a good day," said my grandfather.

I noticed that my grandmother had on a new apron, and my grandfather's blue work shirt had the creases of a shirt that has never been washed. He was the most excited of us all. He hummed little songs in his tuneless way, and his eyes were sharp with the occasion. His sweat made the dark shirt darker under his shoulders and in the middle of his chest. His lean arms were burned, and his bald head was pale when he took off the cloth cap he always wore in the sun. He told how he had helped out, a hired boy, for ten cents a day when he had been my age. The farmer had threatened to charge him for drinks of water, out of the horse trough at the barn, when they brought in their loads of hay. "It's a mighty deep well," the farmer had said, "but you look like to drink it dry, Wesley Wells."

When we had eaten the last pickle and had shaken the crumbs from the quilt, Caroline and my grandmother packed the empty basket and the quilt into the Studebaker. My grandmother told me to watch I didn't take too much sun, and to make sure that Gramp was careful when he turned from the field onto the macadam on the way home. Then they drove off.

I walked back to the apple tree, where my grandfather was stretched out in the shade, taking a shortened version of his rest after lunch. Anson was sitting cross-legged, chewing on a piece of grass. He smiled at me, and I think he was excited too. I sat down beside him.

In a moment my grandfather leapt to his feet, standing so quickly that it seemed there was no intermediate position between lying down and standing up. "Well, now, you jack rabbits!" he said. "Anson, you go draw some water for Riley. Donnie, you come with me and we'll hitch Riley up to the rake." We strode off to the other side of the field, through the swathes of cut hay, to the tree where Riley was tied. Just beyond was a stone fence that separated the field from an old pasture which was growing up with brush and young pine. Riley was old and thin in 1939; his ribs stuck out and there was a sore on his left hip. My grandfather hated to work him, but he had no alternative, and he tried to make up to Riley with apples and sugar and praise.

Now, after he cooed a little at him, he untied Riley's rope and led him over to the big metal horse-rake, and backed him between the shafts. The mowing machine was next to it, leaning on its shafts like two long stiff arms, and the hayrack was just beyond.

My grandfather buckled the leather straps of Riley's harness, and I looked up to see Anson trudging across the field with a big pail of water. Riley leaned his neck into the pail and drank in long, rhythmic swallows. "You'll lose it, old baby, pulling out there in the sun," said my grandfather, and when Riley lifted his dripping jaws from the bucket, my grandfather climbed into the saddle-shaped metal driver's seat, beside the handle which controlled the rake, and moved off to the cut hay.

He raked the hay into even strips, thirty feet apart, that crossed the field parallel to the road. After he had completed three trips up and down, Anson began to rake the strips into small haystacks. He used the bullrake, a great wooden rake about five feet wide with teeth a foot long and four inches apart. I took the tiny rake and trimmed around rocks and trees, getting the hay which my grandfather missed. When I had gathered enough to carry, I pulled it to the nearest strip or haystack. After I had finished with the trimming, I sat in the shade and chewed on pieces of grass.

There were no sounds but the whirr of an occasional car, and the shouts of my grandfather to Riley, "Whoa! Back! Get up!" The sun was high and I was already sweating, but the breeze cooled me off as I sat in the shade. I practiced noticing the details of texture and color around me. That summer I had a theory that if you looked at anything closely enough, it would be beautiful. I examined a blade of grass, its string construction and the layer of gray which seemed to underlie the green.

Soon little haystacks spotted the whole field. My grandfather finished making his long strips before Anson could pile more than a third of the hay; so he drew the rest into piles with the quicker horserake. It took about forty-five minutes to do all the raking.

My grandfather drove Riley next to the hayrack and climbed down from his metal perch. He took his cap off and wiped the sweat from his face and neck and head with a huge handkerchief. "Don't have any hair to catch the sweat with," he said, as I had heard him say often. Riley was finishing the pail of water. My

9

grandfather sat down for a moment in the shade of the hayrack, until Anson walked up to us, pulling the bullrake. "Hot in the sun," my grandfather said. Then he stood and unfastened Riley from the rake and backed him into the shafts of the hayrack. "Time to pull some more hay, old Riley, old baby," he said, and he fastened the straps.

Anson climbed into the hayrack and clucked to get Riley moving toward the nearest pile of hay. "You'll rake after," my grandfather said to me. "You pull the bullrake after us now, and I'll show you what you'll be doing." We walked together to the first haystack. Anson

Hay in windrows waiting to be gathered in Okanogan County, Washington. Photo copyright Steve Terrill (WA-3-7-687).

handed my grandfather his pitchfork. My grandfather sank it expertly into the pile of hay and lifted most of it up to Anson, who placed it where he wanted it for his load. The rest of the haystack followed, leaving a scattering of hay too small to be picked up by a fork. Anson clucked, and Riley automatically began to move toward the nearest stack.

My grandfather let his fork drop. "Now this is what you do, boy," he said. He took the bullrake and in a few turns of the rake he had skillfully gathered the strands of hay left at the site of the pile. "See how to hold it?" he said. I thought I did, but when I first held the rake, he had to rearrange my hands for me. The difficulty was to keep the long teeth flat on the ground, neither pointing up and missing the hay nor pointing down and losing the hay in bounces. I managed to pull the wisp of hay over to the next pile, where Anson, who had jumped down from the wagon to pitch on, incorporated it in his next forkful. Then Anson climbed back up, my grandfather finished pitching the new pile on the rack, and I raked after, while they moved on. I was careful not to miss a single fragment, and I caught up with them just in time for my grandfather to pitch up what I had scavenged.

Anson packed and stowed and treaded the hay with the rote skill of forty years, building the load at the edges evenly back and front, so that the hay leaned out way over the rails, but was fastened securely by forkfuls treaded into the middle. The floor of the rack was only one plank wide near the front where it was cut by wells into which the wheels banked on a sharp turn. The single plank rested on the beam which was the wagon's main support, and to which the axles were attached. (I remember, from my early childhood, the late spring when my grandfather and Washington Woodward built the hayrack; the floor was thick boards bought from a lumber mill, but the rails were split birch, and the spokes which joined the rail to the floor were sticks with the bark still on them.) In loading the hay, it was tricky to cover the wells so that you could walk over them without losing hay, or even falling through yourself. At least it was tricky for me, when in later years I loaded for my grandfather.

Fifteen of the piles filled the old rack. Anson treaded the last two into the middle as binders, and we were ready to take the load home to the cow barn. I must have been hurrying with my raking, for I had forgotten to pay attention to what I was doing; when my rake stuck, I tugged at it and one of the foot-long teeth broke off. For a moment, in my chagrin, I wanted to hide it, but I knew that there would be no hiding it for long. I raked over to my grandfather. "I broke a tooth. The rake stuck in a skunk hole or something."

He laughed. "I reckon we'll have to take it out of your wages." He put the broken tooth in his long overall pocket and I went back to raking after the last pile. When I finished, my grandfather picked up the whole rake and swung it over his head, so that the hay did not fall from it, and laid the final strip of hay across the back of the load, like a narrow fringe of curls on a girl's forehead.

We left the rake and the rest of the equipment behind us, along with considerable hay, and climbed into the wagon by the hub and the rim of a huge front wheel. For this ride, my grandfather handled the reins, while Anson dangled his legs over the back of the rack and sucked on a piece of hay. My grandfather said he loaded himself there to keep the rest of the hay in place. Only a few pieces of hay scattered behind us as we started home, leaving a trail which the cars soon dispersed. Riley walked deliberately, and needed no direction. The cars zipped past us impatiently, but we paid no attention to their haste. It was the opposite of everything in Connecticut, to sit, sinking, in a pile of hay, while a bony old horse pulled a load of hay in a homemade rack along a New Hampshire road at three miles an hour. The smell of the hay was as great a pleasure as the softness of it, and I was full of the joy of haying.

11

June's Eden

HAL BORLAND

Even Adam must have known in June that banishment from Eden was not an undiluted punishment, for surely Eden spilled its fields and gardens, its meadows and woodlands, out beyond the boundaries. As we walked through the June countryside today I knew in my heart that Eden endures, even today. I knew that faith endures, and reasons for it, and that with faith and hope all things are possible.

Daisies now whiten the meadows, and the oriole sings, and the slow turning of the earth is a part of the great current of time, which flows everywhere and forever. Change is like the leaf that spreads to catch the sun. The leaves clothe the earth while time flows, here and in Maine and Dakota and the Carolinas and even in the mesa country of New Mexico. The season we call June comes, and comes again and again, in all its fullness. I have seen June on the mountain tops and in the steaming lower valleys, and nowhere that I know of in this hemisphere is it less than a touch of perfection.

My theology is flexible, and to me Eden may be a memory or a legend; but I know that the Eden of June is very real and is mine for the knowing and the taking. It will be here, waiting, as long as there are men here to enjoy it, and probably long after.

13

A horse relaxing in a field of daisies in Martha's Vineyard, Massachusetts. Photo copyright William H. Johnson, Johnson's Photography (22275-00819).

Little Men and Their Crops

LOUISA MAY ALCOTT

To every thing there is a season, and a time to every purpose under the heaven: A time to be born, and a time to die; a time to plant, and a time to pluck up that which is planted. —ECCLESIASTES 3:1-2

The gardens did well that summer, and in September the little crops were gathered in with much rejoicing. Jack and Ned joined their farms and raised potatoes, those being a good salable article. They got twelve bushels, counting little ones and all, and sold them to Mr. Bhaer at a fair price, for potatoes went fast in that house. Emil and Franz devoted themselves to corn, and had a jolly little husking in the barn, after which they took their corn to the mill, and came proudly home with meal enough to supply the family with hasty-pudding and Johnny-cake for a long time. They would not take money for their crop; because, as Franz said, "We never can pay Uncle for all he has done for us if we raised corn for the rest of our days."

Nat had beans in such abundance that he despaired of ever shelling them, till Mrs. Jo proposed a new way, which succeeded admirably. The dry pods were spread upon the barn floor, Nat fiddled, and the boys danced quadrilles on them, till they were thrashed out with much merriment and very little labor.

Tommy's six weeks' beans were a failure; for a dry spell early in the season hurt them, because he gave them no water; and after that he was so sure that they could take care of themselves, he let the poor things struggle with bugs and weeds till they were exhausted, and died a lingering death. So Tommy had to dig his farm over again, and

Ripe blackberries waiting to be picked in Bristol, New Hampshire. Photo copyright William H. Johnson, Johnson's Photography (33015-00102).

plant peas. But they were late; the birds ate many; the bushes, not being firmly planted, blew down, and when the poor peas came at last, no one cared for them, as their day was over, and spring lamb had grown into mutton. Tommy consoled himself with a charitable effort; for he transplanted all the thistles, he could find, and tended them carefully for Toby, who was fond of the delicacy, and had eaten all he could find on the place. The boys had great fun over Tom's thistles; but he insisted that it was better to care for poor Toby than for himself and declared that he would devote his entire farm next year to thistles, worms, and snails, that Demi's turtles and Nat's pet owl might have the food they loved, as well as the donkey. So like shiftless, kind-hearted, happy-go-lucky Tommy!

Demi had supplied his grandmother with lettuce all summer, and in the autumn sent his grandfather a basket of turnips, each one scrubbed up till it looked like a great white egg. His Grandma was fond of salad, and one of his Grandpa's favorite quotations was:

> Lucullus, whom frugality could charm,
> Ate roasted turnips at the Sabine farm.

Therefore these vegetable offerings to the dear domestic god and goddess were affectionate, appropriate and classical.

Daisy had nothing but flowers in her little plot, and it bloomed all summer long with a succession of gay or fragrant posies. She was very fond of her garden, and delved away in it at all hours, watching over her roses, and pansies, sweet-peas, and mignonette, as faithfully and tenderly as she did over her dolls or her friends. Little nosegays were sent into town on all occasions, and certain vases about the house were her especial care. She had all sorts of pretty fancies about her flowers, and loved to tell the children the story of the pansy, and show them how the step-mother-leaf sat up in her green chair in purple and gold; how her two own children in

gay yellow had each its little seat, while the stepchildren, in dull colors, both sat on one small stool, and the poor little father, in his red nightcap, was kept out of sight in the middle of the flower; that a monk's dark face looked out of the monk's-hood larkspur; that the flowers of the canary-vine were so like dainty birds fluttering their yellow wings, that one almost expected to see them fly away, and the snapdragons that went off like little pistol-shots when you cracked them. Splendid dollies did she make out of scarlet and white poppies, with ruffled robes tied round the waist with grass blade sashes and astonishing hats of coriopsis on their green heads. Pea-pod boats, with rose-leaf sails, received these flower-people and floated them about a placid pool in the most charming style; for finding that there were no elves, Daisy made her own, and loved the fanciful little friends who played their parts in her summer life.

Nan went in for herbs, and had a fine display of useful plants, which she tended with steadily increasing interest and care. Very busy was she in September cutting, drying, and tying up her sweet harvest, and writing down in a little book how the different herbs are to be used.

Dick, Dolly, and Rob each grubbed away on his small farm, and made more stir about it than all the rest put together. Parsnips and carrots were the crops of the two D.'s; and they longed for it to be late enough to pull up the precious vegetables. Dick did privately examine his carrots, and planted them again, feeling that Silas was right in saying it was too soon for them yet.

Rob's crop was four small squashes and one immense pumpkin. It really was a "bouncer," as every one said; and I assure you that two small persons could sit on it side by side. It seemed to have absorbed all the goodness of the little garden, and all the sunshine that shone down on it, and lay there a great round, golden ball, full of rich suggestions of pumpkin pies for weeks to come. Robby was so proud of his mammoth vegetable that he took every one to see it, and, when frosts began to nip, covered it up each night with an old bed quilt, tucking it round as if the pumpkin was a well-beloved baby. The day it was gathered he would let no one touch it but himself, and nearly broke his back tugging it to the barn in his little wheelbarrow, with Dick and Dolly harnessed in front to give a heave up the path. His mother promised him that the Thanksgiving pies should be made from it, and hinted vaguely that she had a plan in her head which would cover the prize pumpkin and its owner with glory.

Poor Billy had planted cucumbers, but unfortunately hoed them up and left the pigweed. This mistake grieved him very much for ten minutes, then he forgot all about it, and sowed a handful of bright buttons which he had collected, evidently thinking that they were money, and would come up and multiply, so that he might make many quarters, as Tommy did. No one disturbed him, and he did what he liked with his plot, which soon looked as if a series of small earthquakes had stirred it up. When the general harvest day came, he would have had nothing but stones and weeds to show, if kind old Asia had not hung half a dozen oranges on the dead tree he had stuck up in the middle. Billy was delighted with his crop; and no one spoiled his pleasure in the little miracle which pity wrought for him, by making withered branches bear strange fruit.

Stuffy had various trials with his melons; for, being impatient to taste them, he had a solitary revel before they were ripe, and made himself so ill, that for a day or two it seemed doubtful if he would ever eat any more. But he pulled through it, and served up his first cantaloupe without tasting a mouthful himself. They were excellent melons, for he had a warm slope for them, and they ripened fast. The last and best

were lingering on the vines, and Stuffy had announced that he should sell them to a neighbor. This disappointed the boys, who had hoped to eat the melons themselves.

Dan had no garden, for he was away or lame the greater part of the summer; so he had helped Silas wherever he could, chopped wood for Asia, and taken care of the lawn so well, that Mrs. Jo always had smooth paths and nicely shaven turf before her door.

When the others got in their crops, he looked sorry that he had so little to show; but as autumn went on, he bethought him of a woodland harvest which was peculiarly his own. . . .

The great garret was full of the children's little stores, and for a time was one of the sights of the house. Daisy's flower seeds in neat little paper bags, all labeled, lay in the drawer of a three-legged table. Nan's herbs hung in bunches against the wall, filling the air with their aromatic breath. Tommy had a basket of thistle down with the tiny seeds attached, for he meant to plant them next year, if they did not all fly away before that time. Emil had bunches of popcorn hanging there to dry, and Demi laid up acorns and different sorts of grain for the pets. But Dan's crop made the best show, for fully one half of the floor was covered with the nuts he brought. All kinds were there, for he ranged the woods for miles round, climbed the tallest trees, and forced his way into the thickest hedges for his plunder. Walnuts, chestnuts, hazelnuts, and beechnuts lay in separate compartments, getting brown, and dry, and sweet, ready for winter revels.

Father and Mother Bhaer's crop was of a different sort, and not so easily described; but they were satisfied with it, felt that their summer work had prospered well, and by and by had a harvest that made them very happy.

Stone Walls

FRANK FARRINGTON

A stone wall is one of the best of companions, and if there is any walk that breeds an outdoor love, it is that which follows the wall's rambling route, where the goldenrod rallies in greatest numbers its gilded guidons, where the briers seek protection against the ruthless blade of the destroying scythe, and where the chipmunk finds a broad and unobstructed highway leading to the woods.

Along its course one may wander with a safe assurance of a pleasant seat for a rest when the spirit bids one stop and muse upon the glow of sunlight on a distant hilltop or upon the song of the rustling leaves in the poplar grove.

Anyone can clamber over a stone wall. It forms no prohibitory boundary for the walker, and yet it restrains even the most ambitious sheep and forms such an imperishable indication of the limit of ownership as outlasts the memory of generations.

The old stone walls of eastern Massachusetts, dating back to the Battle of Concord and Lexington days, are a part of the history of our country. Those of other states, notably the South, are no less so. What a pity that they must all disappear to be replaced by spick-and-span barbed wires, the enemy of stock and the despair of cross-lots travelers!

In the stone wall we have a link that helps to bind the past of our fathers to the future of our children. Its gradual extinction may serve to remind us that the necessities of civilization are slowly driving into the background a thousand artifices that have long contributed a great deal of pleasure to lovers of the outdoors, making clear the fact that though we enjoy much by living in the commercial present, on the other hand, we miss much of which the vagabond of the past was possessor.

Flower in a Crannied Wall

Flower in the crannied wall,
I pluck you out of the crannies,
I hold you here, root and all, in my hand,
Little flower—but *if* I could understand
What you are, root and all, and all in all,
I should know what God and man is.

ALFRED, LORD TENNYSON

Sugar maple tree and autumn leaves beside a stone wall in Amherst, New Hampshire. Photo copyright William H. Johnson, Johnson's Photography (23094-02719).

Mountain Rivers

JOHN MUIR

Most people like to look at mountain rivers. . . . After tracing the Sierra streams from their fountains to the plains, marking where they bloom white in falls, glide in crystal plumes, surge gray and foam-filled in boulder choked gorges, and slip through the woods in long, tranquil reaches—after thus learning their language and forms in detail, we may at length hear them chanting all together in one grand anthem and comprehend them all in clear inner vision, covering the range like lace.

The Green Pasture

ALDO LEOPOLD

Some paintings become famous because, being durable, they are viewed by successive generations, in each of which are likely to be found a few appreciative eyes.

I know a painting so evanescent that it is seldom viewed at all, except by some wandering deer. It is a river who wields the brush, and it is the same river who, before I can bring my friends to view his work, erases it forever from human view. After that it exists only in my mind's eye.

Like other artists, my river is temperamental; there is no predicting when the mood to paint will come upon him, or how long it will last. But in midsummer, when the great white fleets cruise the sky for day after flawless day, it is worth strolling down to the sandbars just to see whether he has been at work.

Horses in a summer meadow bordering Little Sheep Creek in Wallowa County, Oregon. Photo copyright Steve Terrill (OR-7-7-391).

The Garden

BEN LOGAN

God Almighty first planted a garden; and, indeed, it is the purest of human pleasures. —FRANCIS BACON

When the birds came back in the spring, Mother began to think about her garden. Out came the seeds—store-bought ones in neat little packages and those we had harvested last fall in unused Sears and Montgomery Ward order envelopes. With the packets spread around her at the dining-room table, she would shut her eyes and see the garden in front of her, then make a list of any additional seeds she needed.

The garden was a little field west of the house. Father was in charge of the rest of the land, but that little field was hers alone. I don't know how Mother decided when the time was right to begin. Maybe it was mostly a matter of when she could get to it. Maybe there were observations or signs that told her, so that a day would suddenly be the right one. Only now does it occur to me that the day always seemed to come on Saturday when I was out of school.

However it happened, she would announce at breakfast one morning that she wanted the garden spread with manure, then plowed and harrowed. It was always a surprise, maybe even to her, and she always meant today if at all possible. Father planned his work far ahead, so there was never really a right time for garden preparation. He would sigh, and we could see him reshuffling things inside his head before he said, "All right. We'll do it right after breakfast."

Mother would smile and say, "Thank you."

He would smile back, and there was something in the air between them, close and private, that made us stay very still.

For some reason it was always Lyle who got the garden ready, even though it made him feel foolish to be using the big horses and heavy equipment on such a little piece of land. "Heck and tooter," he would say, "the garden's so short I have to yell 'get ep' and 'ho' at the same time to keep from going right through the house."

Because I was the youngest and smallest, I worked

more with Mother than my brothers did. For as long as I can remember, she and I planted the garden, though I'm sure my brothers had a turn, one by one, before me. There was a close warmth in it, a sense of being important and needed, knowing that I was a partner with her and the soil, sun, and rain in helping things grow and putting food on the table. Later, when I went out to get radishes, lettuce, and carrots for a meal, the smile of delight on Mother's face as I brought them in was the kind of payment that made me feel I'd grown an inch.

We were a busy family. Rarely did we sit down just for the sake of sitting and talking. Even meals tended to be rather silent. But when we worked together there was time for talk. It might begin casually, but when you are working with the soil, the plants, and the seasons, any conversation can lead you into philosophy.

It was in planting the garden that I felt closest to Mother. Despite the hard work, I was always sorry when the job was done and I could go back to other things. Partly, I suppose, it was a way of being something the youngest rarely is—an only child, with her undivided attention.

We began the garden by stretching a strong string across it near the north end, the cord lined up with a west window of the house on one side, with a plum tree on the other side. The section to the north of the cord we left alone. It was for volunteers, where seeds from last year's tomatoes and ground cherries would germinate and push up to the surface in the freshly turned soil. Volunteers that appeared in other parts of the garden would be transplanted there.

Under the string, we raked the surface smooth, then made a shallow furrow with the corner of a hoe for our first row of seeds. Here a side of Mother appeared that was like Father. She did not have to look at the seed packages or in a book to see how far apart the rows should be, how close together to drop the seeds, how deep to cover. She was, though, a little more on the side of the extravagant maple tree than Father was. She liked to plant a few extra seeds, "just to be sure," and thin the plants after they came up.

It was all very personal, the planting. Each seed passed through the warmth of our hands. It was a thing to be done with great responsibility, this taking of living seeds from the envelopes where they had lain dormant and putting them properly into the soil so they could awake and grow. It had the richness of an annual ritual.

Putting in the Seed

You come to fetch me from my work to-night
When supper's on the table, and we'll see
If I can leave off burying the white
Soft petals fallen from the apple tree
(Soft petals, yes, but not so barren quite,
Mingled with these, smooth bean and wrinkled pea;)
And go along with you ere you lose sight
Of what you came for and become like me,
Slave to a springtime passion for the earth.
How Love burns through the Putting in the Seed
On through the watching for that early birth
When, just as the soil tarnishes with weed,

The sturdy seedling with arched body comes
Shouldering its way and shedding the earth crumbs.

ROBERT FROST

Fables and Flowers

MEL ELLIS

During July, midway through the flowering seasons, may be a good time to reflect on how the world of wild plants has played such an important part in so many societies. Yesteryear, quarreling couples did not seek out a marriage counselor, but gathered wood betony and, wearing it as a love balm, lived happily ever after. Menominee Indian men believed sneaking flowers of the Indian paintbrush among a fair maid's clothing would make her enamored of him.

Beads of the rosary were once made from the hard seeds of the common hoary puccoon; and the common stinging nettle, thrown into the fireplace, was insurance against a lightning strike during a storm. Roadside yarrow was a base for tea, to dispel melancholia in the inhabitants of the Orkney Islands. It was also used . . . as a vinegar ingredient in Switzerland and as part of an ointment that healed wounded soldiers at the siege of Troy.

Blackberries were recommended to make loose teeth fast again, catnip was used as a soothing syrup for babies, and Solomon's seal . . . was supposed to knit broken bones. Broth from the cleavers, whose stiff bristles have vexed many an American barefoot boy, was supposed to make a fat person thin . . . .

The common white water Lily was thought to have grown from a fallen star, and the chicory, found along every roadside, is an Austrian maiden who vowed never to cease grieving for a lover lost in the war until she was turned into a flower. These, and hundreds of others, are the tales which tell how once the world of flowers played an important role in all except today's modern society. So drive slowly some hot July, where the chicory is thick as patches of blue sky, and perhaps you will hear the lovelorn maiden sigh, even though she sounds a little like the wind.

A Water-Lily at Evening

Sleep, lily, on the lake,
  Without one troubled dream
Thy hushed repose to break,
  Until the morning beam
Shall open thy glad heart again
To live its life apart from pain.

So still in thy repose,
  So pure thy petals seem,
As heaven would here disclose
  Its peace, and we might deem
A soul in each white lily lay
Passionless, from the lands of day.

F. W. BOURDILLON

Wild lily-of-the-valley growing near Bristol, New Hampshire. Photo copyright William H. Johnson, Johnson's Photography (53098-00208).

Pray, Love, Remember...

BERNITA HARRIS

And 'tis my faith that every flower
Enjoys the air it breathes.

–WILLIAM WORDSWORTH

Remember the smells of grandmother's house? The delicious downstairs smells of pickles and apple pie and lemon polish? But there were upstairs smells, too, and the best smell of all was the captivating scent of the starched white sheets and lace-edged, hand-embroidered pillow cases stacked in grandmother's linen closet, or smoothed under quilts and coverlets on the guest chamber beds.

Sweet smelling flowers and herbs have been used for centuries to delight the dreams of families and friends. Here are five of the most fragrant which you can grow in your garden, in window boxes, or in pretty pots in a sunlit space.

If nostalgia could be distilled to a perfume, then that essence would be lavender. "Lavender blue, dilly, dilly, Lavender green, When I am king, dilly, dilly, You shall be queen," promises an old nursery rhyme. Lavender has always been the most popular flower for perfuming linen closets.

Lavandula spica grows about two feet high, with gray-green curling leaves and pale violet flowers on a terminal stalk. Propagated by cuttings and root division, it likes a dry, light, limy soil. Since the plants are not truly hardy, they should be protected by mulching in northern areas over the winter.

Verbena, meaning "sacred bough," is sometimes known by its antique name "vervain." . . . it was also used . . . by herbalists as a cure for everything from jaundice to miscarriage.

Verbena hortensis is another "tender perennial" (therefore an annual in the north.) It blooms continuously from June to late fall, producing white, red, or lilac flowers in broad, flat clusters, eight inches high. The seeds may be sown in sunny window boxes and then transplanted in May, or sown directly in the garden in April or May. It also is best increased by cuttings, usually taken in September and rooted in moist sand in the spring. Ideal for edgings, window boxes, rock gardens, it makes excellent ground cover for summer and fall bulbs.

Sweet Marjoram was said to have been planted on

THE IDEALS COUNTRY TREASURY

Mount Olympus by Venus herself. It's a shame that the goddess's choice should so often be banished to the kitchen and used merely to flavor soups and salads!

Majorana hortensis grows well in window boxes or as a pot plant, if kept on the dry side and given plenty of light. A bushy herb, growing twelve to eighteen inches high, it produces dainty white, pale pink or lavender flowers. It is also a tender perennial. For the garden, sow seeds in flats shielded from strong sun and transplant in late spring.

Rosemary is another shrub of many legends. Folklore tells us that rosemary will not grow in the garden of anyone who is unkind or unfaithful. It has always been a lover's charm. Of course, the best known reference to this perennial bush is found in Shakespeare's *Hamlet*, where the fair and poignant Ophelia pleads: "There's rosemary; that's for remembrance; pray, love, remember."

Rosmarinus officinalis grows about four feet tall with silvery green, needle-shaped leaves, and grows equally well in garden, pot, or tub. It should be pruned often to keep it bushy.

Roses are a book unto themselves. Sacred to Isis, just for an instance, they are closely associated with the culture of many civilizations. Beloved by callow youths and their enamoratas, the bane of poetry editors, the rose figures in religion, heraldry, customs and legends and is prominent in all the arts from architecture to music. My grandmother gathered her roses from a bush which grew amid ribbon grass and sunken flagstones just outside her front door.

Roses are so widely known and widely grown, it would be impertinent here to give any directions on their cultivation.

If you don't have the time or space to grow your own, these flowers and herbs can be bought in bulk. Raid your spice cabinet or supermarket shelves for rosemary and marjoram. Many department stores sell rose petals and lavender. Other sources are health food stores, specialty food shops, farmer's markets, and spice and condiment outlets.

For drying, pick your blooms and leaves in the morning when the dew is off but before the sun is high. Spread them out on racks or in shallow pans in a dry, warm place, turning every now and then until they are dry enough to crumble. Another method is to put a cup or two of leaves or petals in a large, brown paper bag, twist the top tightly and keep in a cupboard until dry. When dry, store them as you would any herb in tightly stopped glass bottles away from light.

For sachets: Cut four thicknesses of colored net in six-inch squares. Fill with one-half cup flowers and tie with ribbon. These are nice for closets and chests. Sew plain gingham bags and pin them to your pillows; or make fat, flat velvet packets about four inches square and trim with lace to lie among your linens, on your shelves, or in your dresser drawers.

Use the dried flowers singly for individual impact or make a potpourri.

To make enough for six to eight sachets, combine one cup lavender or verbena, one-half cup rosemary, one-half cup sweet marjoram, and one cup rose petals.

I have two of my grandmother's sachets. They are crocheted in the shape of hearts, with matching satin linings and satin ribbons threaded through. One is pink, and bears the lingering fragrance of rose petals; the other is blue and still redolent of lavender.

The sachets evoke memories of an era of gentle grace and elegance: of oval mirrors in carved rosewood frames, of pitcher and basin sets decorated with forget-me-nots and roses, of a time when attention to guests included a scented pillow to banish heartache and summon sweet rest.

Sweet memories. Sweet dreams.

27

The Flower

Once in a golden hour
    I cast to earth a seed.
Up there came a flower,
    The people said, a weed.

Then it grew so tall
    It wore a crown of light,
But thieves from o'er the wall
Stole the seed by night;

Sowed it far and wide
    By every town and tower,
Till all the people cried,
    "Splendid is the flower."

ALFRED, LORD TENNYSON

The Lord God Planted a Garden

The Lord God planted a garden
    In the first white days of the world,
And he set there an angel warden
    In a garment of light enfurled.

So near to the peace of Heaven,
    That the hawk might nest with the wren,
For there in the cool of the even
    God walked with the first of men.

The kiss of the sun for pardon,
    The song of the birds for mirth—
One is nearer God's heart in a garden
    Than anywhere else on earth.

DOROTHY FRANCES GURNEY

28

A FLORAL GARDEN OF VERSE

Lovely flowers
are smiles of
God's goodness.

–SAMUEL WILBERFORCE

Red and White

Nobody picks a red rose when the winter wind howls and the
    white snow blows among the fences and storm doors.
Nobody watches the dreamy sculptures of snow when the summer
    roses blow red and soft in the garden yards and corners.
O I have loved red roses and O I have loved white snow—
    dreamy drifts winter and summer—roses and snow.

CARL SANDBURG

To the Fringed Gentian

Thou blossom, bright with autumn dew,
And colored with the heaven's own blue,
That openest when the quiet light
Succeeds the keen and frosty night;

Thou comest not when violets lean
O'er wandering brooks and springs unseen,
Or columbines, in purple dressed,
Nod o'er the ground-bird's hidden nest.

Thou waitest late, and com'st alone,
When woods are bare and birds are flown,
And frosts and shortening days portend
The aged year is near his end.

Then doth thy sweet and quiet eye
Look through its fringes to the sky,
Blue—blue—as if that sky let fall
A flower from its cerulean wall.

WILLIAM CULLEN BRYANT

As for marigolds, poppies, hollyhocks, and valorous sunflowers, we shall never have a garden without them.

—HENRY WARD BEECHER

Flowers are the beautiful hieroglyphics of nature, with which she indicates how much she loves us. —J. W. VON GOETHE

Wild Flowers

How thick the wild flowers blow about our feet,
Thick strewn and unregarded, which, if rare,
We should take note how beautiful they were,
How delicately wrought, of scent how sweet.
And mercies which on every path we meet,
Whose very commonness should win more praise,
Do for that very cause less wonder raise,
And these with slighter thankfulness we greet.
Yet pause thou often on life's onward way,
Pause time enough to stoop and gather one
Of these sweet wild flowers—time enough to tell
Its beauty over; this when thou hast done,
And marked it duly, then if thou canst lay
It wet with thankful tears into thy bosom, well!

RICHARD CHENEVIX TRENCH

See how the flowers, as at parade,
Under their colors stand displayed;
Each regiment in order grows,
That of the tulip, pink, and rose.

ANDREW MARVELL

29

Chapter Two

HEARTH
AND
HOME

Granny's Farm

DEBORAH BOONE

The ornament of a house is the friends who frequent it. —RALPH WALDO EMERSON

As a child, the long, hot days of July and August meant two wonderful things—freedom from school and a visit to Granny's farm. From the moment our car pulled into the long, dusty gravel driveway and we saw the big farmhouse with its long white verandah, we experienced a carefree sense of comfort that we never knew back in the city. Our grandmother would be waiting for us with a big smile, a welcoming kiss, and those wonderful words, "You girls go on and have fun!"

It was all fun. First, we climbed the oak and maple trees that shaded the house cooling it in summer. Hanging in one of the trees was an old swing that my mother had used as a a girl, and we took turns swinging as high as we could go. We ran through wild flowers in the meadow, chewed on long pieces of timothy, and braided daisies into chains. After exploring the yard and fields, we ran into the old barn.

The barn was huge and our voices echoed within its caverns. Hanging from wooden pegs were ancient farm implements, tools, horse harnesses—mysterious objects to two city girls, and we played guessing games as to what each item was for. We explored every inch of that barn: up a ladder to the hayloft to swing from an old rope hanging from the rafters. Down below was the cow we fed wisps of hay. Suddenly, around our feet, clucking noisily, were the chickens, often one with baby chicks waddling behind.

Granny always had a few barn cats, and often there was a litter of soft and silky kittens. The little things were so tiny, so soft, and each a different color: black, gray, and yellow. They always knew when Granny set out the dish of milk on the back porch. The soft chant of, "Here, kitty, kitty," brought them running from all over the farm.

Granny assigned us "chores" while we were there. There was no running water on that farm but we didn't mind hauling buckets of water from the pump to the kitchen. The water wouldn't flow, however, until the pump had been primed with a bit of water, saved for that purpose. Then up, and down, up and down, went that long wooden pump handle, the water flowing into the bucket.

When it was time to start dinner, we were sent outside to what seemed to be an endless garden. We picked tender leaf lettuce, a basketful of crisp green beans, pulled ears of corn off the plants, and last, carefully, oh so carefully, picked big, beautiful, red tomatoes, fresh and ripe from the vine.

When it was time to cook, we brought in the kindling and stove-wood for the gigantic white enameled woodstove Granny cooked on. Granny lifted the heavy metal lids and we girls poked the wood into the red-hot interior. There was usually a chicken roasting in the oven along with a blackberry pie. Homemade bread and jam, pickles and relishes, were always on the table and warm oatmeal cookies for, as Granny said, "anyone who didn't like pie." Granny didn't set what she called a "fancy table." The checked cloth covered the big round oak table with the spoons placed in a glass in the middle of the table. While we were there, there would always be another glass with some daisies in it brought from the meadow for our Granny.

At home, we were never ready for bedtime, but on the farm, we collapsed in Granny's big old-fashioned bed, with its white iron frame. Granny tucked us in with a crazy quilt she had made long ago from leftover scraps of clothes. Each night we pointed to the patches in the quilt and Granny would reveal to us her memories—Grandpa's Sunday vest, our mother's favorite school dress, a baby's shirt. We said our prayers, then Granny kissed us good night and turned out the light. As we snuggled down into those crisp white sheets, fresh off the clothesline, we smelled the cool freshness of the country blowing through the open window. We were safe. We were at Granny's house.

Wild poppies line a mountain road with Mt. Hood in the background in Hood River County, Oregon. Photo copyright Steve Terrill (OR-1-5-796).

The Country Kitchen

MAXINE KUMIN

On these small cares of daughter, wife, or friend, The almost sacred joys of home depend. —HANNAH MORE

Conjure up the country kitchen on a hard winter evening, the thermometer falling inexorably, so says the weather report, toward twenty degrees below zero. An hour ago in four P.M. twilight the animals came willingly into the barn to dry bedding, fresh water, sweet feed, and hay. A light snow had begun to swirl through the air in dry eddies. What comfort to slide the latches closed, whistle slavish dog and disdainful cat uphill into the heart of the house! They lie down together on their square of folded rug next to the cooking stove, hostilities suspended until daybreak.

Across the way, where a wall might logically set living room apart from kitchen, homemade vegetable soup thaws on the woodstove. On the hearth, twice-risen loaves of bread rest before being baked. No barrier separates living space from the food and general-activities center of the country house. Indeed, under pressure from a new way of life in which radiant heat from wood-burning stoves must circulate unimpeded by dividers, virtually every house with a chimney today has abandoned the closed-door imperative of the high-technology kitchen.

In winter the kitchen table lends itself to Scrabble games. Between plays, family members are exhorted to pick nut meats from hickories or butternuts. How else will these tedious tasks be done? The kitchen table is the logical place to pore over the new seed catalogue, while a sleet storm ticks against the window. Shall it be elephant garlic, Egyptian onions, the new hybrid squash called Kuta? Here's a new strain of edible Japanese chrysanthemums. The best light and steadiest warmth in the winter house surround the kitchen table. Readings and writings take place here. So do infrequent sewings and, properly protected with old newspapers, cleanings of harness and riding tack. And when the power fails, as it must three or four times a year, all repair to the kitchen table with the Family Lamp, readied against such emergencies with kerosene and neatly trimmed wick.

34

Where does the insomniac go? The mother or, increasingly, father, with baby at two A.M.? Indeed, not only does the dog lie down with the cat here, but in February enters the orphan lamb in an abused playpen. In March, a dozen new chicks. Once, briefly and by mistake, the wethered goat. Several times, peering mildly through the backdoor screen, the heifers. How disconcerting to raise up your eyes from the pie crust to find those large, sloe-eyed creatures looking in.

The morning kitchen is cheerful and workable, ready for the comfortable dishevelment of coffee brewing, bread slicing, the beating of eggs, the frying of bacon. It is a quiet time, good for elaborate planning of renovation, addition, improvement. The morning kitchen looks out on the rush-hour traffic at the bird feeder. The world is new again; the grosbeaks are back. The morning kitchen belongs to the idealist. . . .

Early in summer, color the country kitchen scarlet, a ripeness streaked with sunlight shading into purple. Rhubarb, the first lifeblood of the season, is ready early in June. Before the month is out, strawberries overtake it. Jam bubbles on the stove, pies drip in the oven. The kitchen becomes a factory of steam and smells, food mills, blanching vessels, tongs, jars, bottles, juices, and purees. It will turn out hundreds of pounds of produce between now and October. Everything surplus, everything homegrown or acquired at the local farmers' market marches into this command post to be dealt with, judiciously divided for present pleasure and future use.

In full summer, color the kitchen green, streaked with yellow. Erect as milkweed, asparagus pops above ground, thickens, and yields to the gatherer's knife. Early peas follow these spears into the freezer. Raspberries, plump and purpling, obedient to the calendar, come next. One blink of the eye and the bush beans, both yellow and green, are in. Mornings of stemming and blanching for the freezer. Half a sigh later, the Kentucky Wonders swarm up their tepees. The repetitive tasks are humbling. We all succumb to the benevolent tyranny of the garden as the first broccoli, the early cauliflower, a crowd of young lettuces overfill the kitchen, waiting to be sorted out. These to be consumed on the spot, those to be blanched and frozen, this to be canned, salted, pickled: all hands to the cutting board and colander.

Green and red and yellow, the summer kitchen is never empty. Cherries pop their pits. Beets bleed, undergoing purification. So alarming is the propensity of summer squash and zucchini to create a glut that entire cookbooks have been devoted to ingenious methods for disposing of them. Suddenly in mid-July the cucumbers arrive, slyly swelling under the protective mat of foliage.

The kitchen shifts into high gear. Bouquets of fresh dill shower the tabletop with yellow crumbs of blossom. Basil, waiting to be buzzed into pesto in the blender, adds its lemony fragrance to an overall scent of vinegar and sugar, spices and earth smells. Peaches enter the marketplace. A bushel or two waits at the foot of the cellar stairs. Evenings, they rise, along with plums, to be halved and packed tight into jars. Two or three successive batches are covered with sugar syrup, submerged in the hot-water bath and boiled the allotted time. Next day, they adorn the winter shelves. Although the pears are still green on the tree, the red squirrels have found them, and the fruit must be picked and processed or all is lost. Blackcaps, arctic cloudberries, and cruelly brambled blackberries, diligently gathered day by day and frozen until a space can be cleared for them, wait to be sieved, sugared, and boiled into jam.

And then all attention is riveted on the corn patch. In spite of our having planted early, midseason, and late varieties, nature conspires to bring the entire crop in at once. For three glorious hedonistic weeks we will dine on it nightly. We rush it from field to pot to table in under ten minutes and save the shucks for horses and heifers. Color the kitchen buttery yellow once the corn comes in. Any we can't eat on the spot is cut from the cob and sped into the freezer.

On hottest nights, color the kitchen crepuscular, only one light glowing, all harvest activities suspended. Consider those eight P.M. suppers with half a dozen fresh vegetables providing the main course. A generous salad based on three varieties of lettuce is overlaid with cukes, carrots, bits of broccoli, and icicles of raw kohlrabi, decorated with crumbs of feta cheese and buttered croutons. Hotter than ever tomorrow? Buzz the leftovers in the blender for cold lunchtime soup.

All too soon the first frost threatens. Gardens grow ghostly under their sheets and old drop cloths; forestalled for a week or two, Jack Frost returns. All over town the green tomatoes come indoors. In every kitchen arises the acrid tang of green-tomato pickle, chutney, chili; on every south-facing kitchen windowsill the most promising greenies line up to be coaxed ripe.

The ultimate reward, October, is celebrated with apples. Given the right degree of overlap, apples and green tomatoes will combine in the kitchen factory to create chutney. But apples alone account for pies and applesauce, cider and apple butter, cores, peels, and pomaces, enough to restore the country kitchen to its best level of frenzied disorder. Peelings for the animals, pomace for compost, quarts of applesauce set aside for winter.

Last, see the kitchen as history. In the all-important larder—in our case, shelves built into the capacious cellar entryway—stand jars full of fruits, pickles, jams, and jellies to stave off the megrims of those twenty-below-zero nights. Peanut butter jars, still wearing the faint imprint on their lids of their sale prices, bespeak a kinder time, when the standard one-pound item sold for sixty-nine cents. That same jar, now full of homemade strawberry, blackberry, plum, or grape jelly or jam, reads $1.19, $1.69, $2.09, $2.89! What's this? asks the archaeologist in the years 3000, $4.65? A dissertation in the year 3050 . . . will put forth hypotheses explaining the elevation of America's midday spread, this mash of the goober, to the expensive status of anchovy paste.

Here, too, stand old-fashioned Ball jars with wire bales and rubber-ring sealers for their glass lids. Although in the average kitchen these have been largely replaced by the far easier self-sealing metal lids, we are still gamely refilling our golden oldies. Many are inherited jars, handed down from grandmothers on both sides. Some have turned the delicate blue of antique glass and stand on a hanging shelf in the kitchen along with an excavated bottle whose raised letters proclaim SOTTS EMULSION on one side, while on the other a fisherman carries a huge cod on his back. On the opposite wall a framed poster advertises the virtues of the Andes stove, a porcelain monster foursquare on its black bowlegs. "Makes poor cooks good and good cooks better," reads the unabashed slogan.

Not an extravagant claim, its unvarnished declaration suits this country kitchen. Nothing fancy takes place here. Merely the steady rhythm of the life of the farm and the people who live here. Making all seasons better.

Large farmhouse kitchen with wood-burning cookstove. Photo copyright Jessie Walker, Jessie Walker and Associates (00021-01231.0001).

Feather Ticks and Quilts

Helen E. Ouimette

Grandma used duck and goose feathers to make her feather pillows and ticks. She preferred duck feathers to goose. I suspect she thought the ducks with their multicolored green and blue necks prettier than geese. Besides, the geese used to chase me, and an angry goose can be pretty formidable with his wings flapping and his long neck thrust forward ready to nip.

The feather ticks were made of all the feathers saved from geese and ducks which had been killed during the year. . . . Feathers from the different parts of the bird were kept separate. The nice downy ones were used as they were, but the quilly ones, like the wings and tail, were stripped. That is, the down was stripped from the quill.

The feather ticks were used instead of quilts. One under, one atop a straw tick, and one to cover with. There was no heat in the upstairs bedrooms, so we used to burrow under those warm comfortable feather ticks, especially on nights when it was so cold that frost glistened on all the walls. The straw or corn shuck ticks were made by sewing ten yards of blue-and-white ticking together, leaving the center of the top side open. Every couple of days, one of the women would reach into the opening and shake up the straw or corn shucks, whichever material was used.

In March, Grandma would buy yards of unbleached muslin, wet it, and hang it on the line to bleach. She said, "The March winds bleached it out." Out of this muslin she sewed the covers for the feather ticks and pillow cases. She also used this muslin to make sheets. Those sheets had a seam down the center, which "boughten" sheets today don't have. . . .

The feathers she saved during the year weren't just for immediate use. It was the custom to save feathers to make feather pillows for both the children and their grandchildren as they got married. . . . Each of my seven children . . . had a feather pillow and a wool quilt made for them. They loved the wool quilts and feather pillows, but during pillow fights they forgot that the feathers floating around the room were an irreplaceable gift of love.

Canada geese among blooming water lilies close to Marlow, New Hampshire. Photo copyright William H. Johnson, Johnson's Photography (43012-00102).

39

Ice Cream Supper

Susan Childs

The only emperor is the emperor of ice cream. —WALLACE STEVENS

My mother's people were a fun and eccentric lot.

Aunt Lessie, splendidly absentminded, made the best five-layer chocolate cake in the county—when she remembered to add the eggs. Aunt Doe, who crumbled cornbread into a glass of buttermilk each morning of her life, swore that breakfast helped her know which cows would give the most milk on any given day. (No doubt it helped account for her substantial girth as well.) That she constantly feuded with Aunt Hess became the stuff of family legend, since they lived together on the farm my great-grandmother had bequeathed them.

It was to this farm that Momma Jo (she was too young, she insisted, to be called grand anything by me) and I headed every weekend during my childhood summers. Wedged between Cheaha Mountain and the Talladega National Forest, the 250-acre spread had been in the Bradley family since before the Civil War. Here, knee-deep in rural Alabama, I witnessed my first river baptism; here I also attended my one and only tent revival. But as exotic as these events were to my urban, New South sensibility, nothing outshines in my memory the ice cream supper that commenced every Sunday at the Bradley farm.

An ice-cream supper is exactly what the name implies: an early evening meal whose first, middle, and last courses, consist of ice cream. No fried chicken, no mashed potatoes—just ice cream, homemade and plenty of it. Ingredients include fresh fruit, condensed milk, eggs, and lots of sugar. Three to four flavors were the norm, but peach and banana were my favorite.

The ritual never deviated. We kids did all the hand-turning that went into making these confections. Those of us who were old enough to drive went for more rock salt if supplies ran low, which they invariably did. When the moment came to test the "cream," Aunt Hess, our official taster, would either exclaim its perfection, or put down the spoon, indicating more time at the crank.

A country cottage surrounded by hollyhocks and phlox. Photo copyright Jessie Walker, Jessie Walker and Associates (00054-02186.0032).

As the eating commenced, so did the telling of stories. My grandfather, addressing me by my family nickname, usually kicked off the adventure by going straight for the funny bone: "Dudebug, did I ever tell you about the time your grandmother got so mad at me she laid under a crabapple tree and fired a pistol straight up into the branches? Mockin' birds shied away from the crabapple after that—and so did your granddaddy."

The anecdote about Momma Jo seemed like heresy to me, but the teasing, which was nothing if not democratic, embraced our imperfections one and all. Weekly we giggled, too, at Aunt Lessie, who once searched all day for her freshly washed nightgown, her favorite blue one, only to find it nesting among the produce in her refrigerator.

On it went, this offbeat summertime social with its good-natured banter. How it thumbed its nose at the time-honored notion of "no peas, no dessert." How it laughed at the institution of proper and saintly grandmothers and great aunts.

Sweet anarchy was the ice-cream supper, presided over by that outlandish and loving bunch, my mother's people.

Small Farm Home

LAURA INGALLS WILDER

He is the happiest, be he king or peasant, who finds peace in his home. —J. W. VON GOETHE

There is a movement in the United States today, wide-spread, and very far reaching in its consequences. People are seeking after a freer, healthier, happier life. They are tired of the noise and dirt, bad air, and crowds of the cities and are turning longing eyes toward the green slopes, wooded hills, pure running water, and health-giving breezes of the country.

A great many of these people are discouraged by the amount of capital required to buy a farm and hesitate at the thought of undertaking a new business. But there is no need to buy a large farm. A small farm will bring in a good living with less work and worry and the business is not hard to learn.

In a settlement of small farms the social life can be much pleasanter than on large farms, where the distance to the nearest neighbor is so great. Fifteen or twenty families on five-acre farms, will be near enough together to have pleasant social gatherings in the evenings. The women can have their embroidery clubs, their reading clubs, and even the children can have their little parties, without much trouble or loss of time. This could not be done if each family lived on a one-hundred- or two-hundred-acre farm. There is less hired help required on the small farm also, and this makes the work in the house lighter.

I am an advocate of the small farm, and I want to tell you how an ideal home can be made on, and a good living made from, five acres of land.

Whenever a woman's home-making is spoken of, the man in the case is presupposed, and the woman's home-making is expected to consist in keeping the house clean and serving good meals on time, etc. In short, that all of her home-making should be inside the house. It takes more than the inside of the house to make a pleasant home, and women are capable of making the whole home, outside and in, if necessary. She can do so to perfection on a five acre farm by hiring some of the outside work done.

However, our ideal home should be made by a man and a woman together. First, I want to say that a five acre farm is large enough for the support of a family. From $75 to $150 a month, besides a great part of the living, can be made on that size farm from poultry or fruit, or a combination of poultry, fruit, and dairy.

This has been proven by actual experience, so that the financial part of this small home is provided for.

Conditions have changed so much in the country within the last few years that we country women have no need to envy our sisters in the city. We women on the farm no longer expect to work as our grandmothers did.

With the high prices to be had for all kinds of timber and wood, we now do not have to burn wood to save the expense of fuel but can have our oil stove, which makes the work so much cooler in the summer, so much lighter and cleaner. There need be no carrying in of wood and carrying out of ashes with the attendant dirt, dust, and disorder.

Our cream separator saves us hours formerly spent in setting and skimming milk and washing pans, besides saving the large amount of cream that was lost in the old way.

Then there is the gasoline engine. Bless it! Besides doing the work of a hired man outside, it can be made to do the pumping of the water and the churning, turn the washing machine and even run the sewing machine.

On many farms running water can be supplied in the house from springs by means of rams or air pumps, and I know of two places where water is piped into and through the house from springs farther up on the hills. This water is brought down by gravity alone and the only expense is the piping. There are many such places in the Ozark hills waiting to be taken advantage of.

This, you see, supplies water works for the kitchen and bath room simply for the initial cost of putting in the pipes. In one farm home I know, where there are no springs to pipe the water from, there is a deep well and a pump just outside the kitchen door. From this a pipe runs into a tank in the kitchen and from this tank there are two pipes. One runs into the cellar and the other underground to a tank in the barnyard, which is of course much lower than the one in the kitchen.

When water is wanted down cellar to keep the cream and butter cool, a cork is pulled from the cellar pipe by means of a little chain and by simply pumping the pump outdoors, cold water runs into the vat in the cellar. The water already there rises and runs out at the overflow pipe, through the cellar and out at the cellar drain.

When the stock at the barn need watering, the cork is pulled from the other pipe, and the water flows from the tank in the kitchen into the tank in the yard. And always the tank in the kitchen is full of fresh, cold water, because this other water all runs through it. This is a simple, inexpensive contrivance for use on a place where there is no running water.

It used to be that the woman on a farm was isolated and behind the times. A weekly paper was what the farmer read, and he had to go to town to get that. All this is changed. Now the rural delivery brings us our daily papers, and we keep up on the news of the world as well or better than though we lived in the city. The telephone gives us connection with the outside world at all times, and we know what is going on in our nearest town by many a pleasant chat with our friends there.

Circulating libraries, thanks to our state university, are scattered throughout the rural districts, and we are eagerly taking advantage of them.

The interurban trolley lines being built through our country will make it increasingly easy for us to run into town for an afternoon's shopping or any other pleasure. These trolley lines are, and more will be, operated by electric-

ity, furnished by our swift running streams, and in a few years our country homes will be lighted by this same electric power.

Yes indeed, things have changed in the country, and we have the advantages of city life if we care to take them. Besides, we have what it is impossible for the woman in the city to have. We have a whole five acres for our back yard and all outdoors for our conservatory, filled not only with beautiful flowers, but with grand old trees as well, with running water and beautiful birds, with sunshine and fresh air and all wild, free, beautiful things.

The children, instead of playing with other children in some street or alley, can go make friends with the birds on their nests in the bushes, as my little girl used to do, until the birds are so tame they will not fly at their approach. They can gather berries in the garden and nuts in the woods and grow strong and healthy, with rosy cheeks and bright eyes. This little farm home is a delightful place for friends to come for afternoon tea under the trees. There is room for a tennis court for the young people. There are skating parties in the winter, and the sewing and reading clubs of the nearby towns, as well as the neighbor women, are always anxious for an invitation to hold their meetings there.

In conclusion I must say if there are any country women who are wasting their time envying their sisters in the city—don't do it. Such an attitude is out-of-date. Wake up to your opportunities. Look your place over, and if you have not kept up with the modern improvements and conveniences in your home, bring yourself up-to-date. Then take the time saved from bringing water from the spring, setting the milk in the old way, and churning by hand, to build yourself a better social life. If you don't take a daily paper, subscribe for one. They are not expensive and are well worth the price in the brightening they will give your mind and the pleasant evenings you can have reading and discussing the news of the world. Take advantage of the circulating library. Make your little farm home noted for its hospitality and the social times you have there. Keep up with the march of progress for the time is coming when the cities will be the workshops of the world and abandoned to the workers, while the real cultured, social, and intellectual life will be in the country.

Perennial flower garden in full bloom in Portsmouth, New Hampshire. Photo by William H. Johnson, Johnson's Photography (23054-00220).

Home

It takes a heap o' livin' in a house t'make
 it home,
A heap o' sun an' shadder, an' ye sometimes
 have t' roam
Afore ye really 'preciate the things ye
 lef' behind,
An' hunger fer 'em somehow with 'em
 allus on yer mind.

Home ain't a place that gold can buy or
 get up in a minute;
Afore it's home there's got t' be a heap
 o' livin' in it;
Within the walls there's got t' be some
 babies born, and then
Right there ye've got t' bring 'em up
 t' women good, an' men.

Who used t'love 'em long ago, an' trained
 'em jes' t' run
The way they do, so's they would get
 the early mornin' sun;
Ye've got t' love each brick an' stone
 from cellar up t' dome:
It takes a heap o' livin' in a house
 to make it home.

EDGAR A. GUEST

45

Far From the Madding Crowd

It seems to me I'd like to go
Where bells don't ring, nor whistles blow,
Nor clocks don't strike, nor gongs sound,
And I'd have stillness all around.

Not real stillness, but just the trees,
Low whispering, or the hum of bees,
Or brooks faint babbling over stones,
In strangely, softly tangled tones.

Or maybe a cricket or a katydid,
Or the songs of birds in the hedges hid,

Or just some such sweet sound as these,
To fill a tired heart with ease.

If 'tweren't for sight and sound and smell,
I'd like the city pretty well,
But when it comes to getting rest,
I like the country lots the best.

Sometimes it seems to me I must
Just quit the city's din and dust,
And get out where the sky is blue,
And say, now, how does it seem to you?

NIXON WATERMAN

46

POEMS FOR A COUNTRY HOME

In spring I delight you,
In summer I cool you,
In autumn I feed you,
In winter I warm you.

A TREE

Old Quilt

Like swift-winged swallows, her small hands flew,
Dipping and darting the bright thread through,
Over and under the steel flashed true—
Silent staccato and constant rhyme.

And, oh, I wonder—did she divine
That the threads would hold, and the quaint design
Should someday rest on a bed of mine,
Bridging the mystical gulf of time?

BETTY CORNWELL

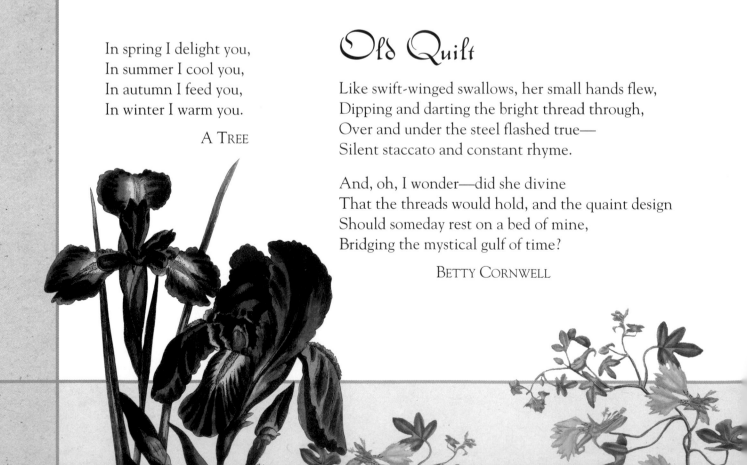

O world, as God has made it! All is beauty. —ROBERT BROWNING

Farm Kitchen at Night

The kettle sings a low contented tune
    The dog snores in her sleep behind the stove,
There is a mingled odor in the air,
    Of apple pie and cinnamon and clove,
The smell of yeast . . . for mother set the bread,
    In the blue pan before she went to bed.

Beyond the pantry door I catch a glimpse
    Of shiny milk pans on a narrow shelf,
A row of plates . . . the old brown cookie crock;
    A brimming water pail all by itself;
A little bracket lamp beside the door,
    Makes a small halo on the kitchen floor.

An old grey cat is sleeping on a chair,
    Paws folded in below her snowy chest;
She looks the picture of contented peace,
    Like an old lady waiting for a guest,
Her eyes blink softly as if half awake,
    Pale green, like water in a mountain lake.

The kitchen has a fragrance of its own,
    Of porridge simmering in a blue pot,
Of kindling wood drying beneath the stove,
    And red coals glowing beautiful and hot;
There is a sense of joy and comfort there,
    In the old stove and cushioned rocking chair.

A feel of home and peace and fireglow,
That lovely modern kitchens do not know.

EDNA JAQUES

Is your place a small place?
Tend it with care!
He set you there.
Is your place a large place?
Guard it with care!
He set you there.
Whate'er your place, it is
Not yours alone, but his
Who set you there.

JOHN OXENHAM

We have careful thought for the stranger,
And smiles for the sometime guest,
But oft for our own the bitter tone,
Though we love our own the best.

MARGARET SANGSTER

The crown of the house is godliness,
The beauty of the house is order.
The glory of the house is hospitality.
The blessing of the house is contentment.

AUTHOR UNKNOWN

Grandma's Dishtowels

LOIS LONNQUIST

A happy family is but an earlier heaven. —JOHN BOWRING

The navy with its system of signal flags and codes has nothing on my Grandma. Grandma's communication was fast, effective, and unique. Grandma's dishtowels dried thousands of dishes throughout the years, but they were also her means of communication with those outside her farmhouse domain.

At exactly twelve noon Grandma would go out to the back porch of her two-story farmhouse and wave her big white dishtowel to my Grandpa and uncles out in the fields. When they saw the waving white towel, they stopped whatever they were doing, waved their straw hats in return, and turned their rigs toward home, hungry from the morning's work. Satisfied that they were on their way, Grandma hurried back inside the kitchen. She filled the big white enamel wash basin with warm water from the cookstove reservoir then took it out on the porch for the men to wash their hands. Returning to the kitchen, she'd slide the pan with freshly made flour biscuits into the hot oven, stir up some gravy, and begin dishing up a hearty meal of beef pot roast, browned potatoes, and fresh green beans and tomatoes. The same wave of Grandma's dishtowel at any other time of the day was a signal for the "menfolks" to rush to the house for some emergency that Grandma could not handle alone. The communication was precise and decidedly low-tech.

The dishtowels that hung in Grandma's kitchen were all made from the sacks purchased each month, filled with the finely ground flour that Grandma used to bake bread each day, biscuits every morning, and pies, cakes, or cookies each afternoon. Once the flour was used up, Grandma split the sack at the seams. She then washed and hung the sack on the line to dry in the sun and the breeze. Once dry, she ironed the cloth, pressing it out flat, then turned in each of the four sides for a double hem, which she stitched on the old treadle sewing machine. Next came the fun part. Grandma would embroider colorful flowers in one corner of the towel—sometimes she embroidered large red roses or orange poppies or tiny pink roses, like modern miniature rose bushes. Grandma liked bright colors on her towels. I even remember one towel with purple blossoming chives. The towel was ironed again and folded into a neat square to be stacked with the others in the kitchen drawer. Ordinary dishtowels were hung on little towel racks in the kitchen, but the "waving-towel" always hung right by the back door.

My brother, sister and I, on our two-mile trek home from our country school, would watch for her. The days that we saw her there, waving her dishtowel, we excitedly waved back. We then turned off our trail to run across the pasture down to the winding little creek, where we skipped across the stepping stones, and hurried up the hill to our grandparent's big white house. Grandma was there with a smile and open arms. She invited us inside for lemonade or hot cocoa, depending upon the season, along with bread, just coming out of the oven, slathered with freshly churned butter. Nothing could have tasted so wonderful. Sitting there, around Grandma's extra long homemade dining table, we ate and laughed and talked about our school days, our homework, the triumphs and disappointments of school life.

Many years have passed since those happy days, but I still have one of Grandma's dishtowels, slightly worn but ironed, folded, and tucked

Old-fashioned farm windmill and sunflowers near Garfield, Kansas. Photo copyright Steve Terrill (KS-22-8-1436).

49

away among my keepsakes. I have learned that, despite modern conveniences of telephone and e-mail, nothing can compare with the message-sending capabilities of Grandma's dishtowel.

Spring Wind

Your spring wind, Lord, is a bullying boy. It snatches the clothes I am trying to pin on the line and whips them about my face. It grabs the lids of trash barrels and sends them spinning like silver hoops. It yanks the vines like a little girl's braids. It shakes the blossom-laden trees, and the sweet confetti of their petals rains down upon me. Your white clouds rush headlong before it. Your great trees bow and sway. Your flowers bend to its caprice. The wind is a rollicking peddler, crying his wonderful wares, browbeating the world to buy. I love your spring wind, Lord, its bright prancing. It makes me want to dance too, to roll a hoop, throw confetti, gather armloads of flowers (instead of clothes). Your vigor is in it. Your joy is in it. Your infinite lively artistry is in it. Thank you for spring wind, Lord.

Marjorie Holmes

This Place of
Summer Dreams

JEFF RENNICKE

What we desire our children to become, we must endeavor to be before them. —ANDREW COMBE

For years I have been driving past a ramshackle old place outside of town, marveling at the remnants of a grand wraparound front porch—gracefully rounded corners, white-post beams, a view of a little creek. Each time I'd think that someday I should pull over.

Well finally I did, suffering the strange looks of passers-by. Now I find myself stepping onto the abandoned porch, the boards creaking under me. I walk around to every corner, as if looking for something. And maybe I am.

My mind drifts to the memory of my grandmother's wide, big-pillared porch set among elms in Kaukauna, Wisconsin. In those days a front porch was a central part of the house and its daily routine: a catchall for muddy boots, baseball gloves, and bags of tomatoes left by neighbors. It was a command post for parents and grandparents, who kept an eye on us playing in the neighborhood, all the while pretending they weren't watching.

But grandmother's porch was more than that. On rainy days the porch became a playground for us kids, limited only by our imaginations. The railing might be that of an elegant ocean liner, with people on the sidewalk being well-wishers seeing us off. . . .

I find a place where a beam of sunlight has warmed the floorboards and sit wondering how long it's been since I've taken the time to porch-sit. . . .

Since, every once in a while I happen across someone on a porch—an older person gazing down the street, a young mother rocking a baby, or kids playing a game. Each time I want to stop and climb up on the porch with them—just to share the view and enjoy life at the speed of a rocking chair.

A farm home, built in 1878, at sunset on a July evening in Lake County, Leadville, Colorado. Photo copyright Jeff Gnass (24310452).

THE IDEALS COUNTRY TREASURY

Chapter Three

COUNTRY GATHERINGS

Family Reunions

DORI SANDERS

We are all of us echoes, repeating the virtues and character of those among whom we live. —JOSEPH JOUBERT

Summertime was special when I was a child. The peaches were ripe, the watermelons were ready, and kinfolk from all over were expected for the family reunion.

It was a busy time, getting the house ready for all the expected guests. Mama would select the best hens and fryers and pen them up so they wouldn't feed on wild garlic and onions. The cows, including my Starlight, were also specially tended—wild garlic and onion would ruin not only their milk but also the butter churned from it.

Daddy and my brothers would dig chalky clay from the creek beds to make whitewash. Everything from the fireplaces inside the house to the rocks around the flower beds outside received a fresh white coat in anticipation of the big event. On the day before the reunion, long plank tables were built and placed out under the kudzu vine-covered trellis that my daddy had designed to run along side our house. Then, with windows opened to let in the breeze, the cooking began.

A fire burned in the old wood stove all day and into the night. Cakes and pies emerged one after the other and were placed immediately in the "pie safe," a simple wooden cabinet that once stood in the corner of our dining room but was moved to the cooler back porch as soon as my daddy screened it in. True to its name, the cabinet kept pies—and cakes, too—safe not only from flies and other insects but from children as well. Its tin doors, perforated for ventilation, were always locked or securely fastened with a thin rope that defied our efforts to untie it—not that my cousins and I didn't try.

Family reunions lasted for days, and they were filled with feasting and the renewing of family ties. . . . Now years later, my sisters and I still work late into the night getting ready for family reunions. We try to figure out how some of the traditional, heavenly tast-

Country house with gardens and porches hung with flags and bunting. Photo copyright Jessie Walker, Jessie Walker and Associates (00151-02186.0106).

ing foods were made. We always talk about Aunt Vestula's cooking and try out seasonings—a dash of this, a pinch of that, a smidgen of something else. We try to remember, but as the night turns into early morning, we begin to have trouble remembering even Aunt Vestula, much less her recipes.

Yes, family-reunion cooking can be intense. The competition is keen, the demand for originality high. We all want to outdo each other. In the end, though, it all comes together. Somebody always makes the traditional foods. I'll use an old family recipe for chicken and dumplings.

Another relative will bring deviled eggs with caper stuffing, another will arrive with a celery cake. These dishes remind the gathered relatives never to forget the past and always, always to expect some bitter with the sweet, a

caution of long-standing among African-Americans in the South.

At a recent reunion, one cousin followed a really old tradition. Wearing a long flowered dress and a flower-covered straw hat, she circulated among the relatives, handing out pretty handwritten recipes for all the foods she had brought and inviting everyone to dine at her table. . . .

At day's end, as city relatives load up their expensive grills, they study my homemade model—an old oven rack mounted on rocks encircling a bed of lively coals. It may be unsophisticated, but, like many simple things, it does the job. In the country, that's all that really counts.

Mashed Potato Casserole

Makes 8 servings

8 boiling potatoes, pared and cooked to just tender
1 8-ounce package cream cheese, softened
2 eggs, lightly beaten

2 tablespoons all-purpose flour
2 tablespoons minced fresh parsley
2 tablespoons minced fresh chives
Salt and pepper
1 3½-ounce can French-fried onions

Preheat oven to 325° F . Lightly butter a 9 x 11-inch baking dish; set aside. Place cooked potatoes in large bowl of electric mixer; beat until smooth. Add cream cheese; blend well. Add eggs, flour, parsley, chives, and salt and pepper to taste. Turn into a prepared baking dish. Sprinkle onions over the top. Bake, uncovered, or until heated through. Serve hot.

Old-Fashioned Reunion

Country Fried Steak and Milk Gravy

Makes 4 servings

2 pound beef round steak, ½-inch thick
2 eggs
1 cup fine dry bread crumbs
½ teaspoon salt

¼ teaspoon black pepper
¼ cup vegetable oil
2 tablespoons all-purpose flour
1 cup milk

Pound steak with mallet. Cut into 8 serving pieces. In a small bowl, beat eggs. Dip meat in egg and then into bread crumbs. Heat oil and brown meat on both sides. Season with salt and pepper. Cover; turn heat to low and cook 45 to 60 minutes. Remove to a warm platter.

To make gravy, stir flour into pan drippings, blending well. Cook and stir until just light brown. Slowly stir in milk, whisking constantly, until gravy begins to thicken. Add salt to taste. Cook over high heat , stirring constantly, 2 to 3 minutes, adding more milk, if needed. Serve with steak.

COUNTRY CORNBREAD

Makes 6 servings

¼ teaspoon baking soda	1 tablespoon baking powder
1¼ cups buttermilk	¼ teaspoon salt
1 cup yellow cornmeal	2 tablespoons butter, melted
1 cup all-purpose flour	2 tablespoons vegetable oil
3 tablespoons sugar	2 large eggs, lightly beaten

Preheat oven to 375°F. In a small bowl, stir baking soda into buttermilk; set aside. In a large mixing bowl, sift together cornmeal, flour, sugar, baking powder, and salt. Add egg, sugar, and oil, stirring just to mix. Stir milk mixture into cornmeal mixture, stirring only until dry mixture is moistened. (If skillet, place in oven long enough to heat skillet.) Pour batter into a 9-inch greased, round baking pan or a heated iron skillet. Bake 25 minutes, or until golden brown and wooden pick inserted near the center comes out clean. Cut into wedges and serve with butter.

SHOO-FLY PIE

Makes 8 servings

¾ cup all-purpose flour	2 tablespoons vegetable shortening
½ teaspoon ground cinnamon	¾ cup boiling water
⅛ teaspoon ground nutmeg	½ teaspoon baking soda
⅛ teaspoon ground ginger	½ cup molasses
⅛ teaspoon ground cloves	1 egg yolk, well beaten
½ cup packed brown sugar	1 unbaked 9-inch pie shell
½ teaspoon salt	Sweetened whipped cream

Preheat oven to 400° F. In a large mixing bowl, combine flour, cinnamon, nutmeg, ginger, cloves, brown sugar, and salt; blend well. Add shortening; mix with fork or pastry blender until consistency of coarse crumbs. Set aside. In a small bowl, combine water and baking soda; stir to dissolve baking soda. Stir in molasses and egg yolk; blend well. Pour molasses mixture into prepared pie shell. Sprinkle brown sugar-flour mixture evenly over top. Bake for 10 minutes then reduce the heat to 325° F. Bake an additional 15 to 20 minutes or until center is firm. Cool on wire rack. Serve with sweetened whipped cream.

The One-Room Schoolhouse

Talbert A. Pond

A teacher affects eternity; he can never tell where his influence stops. —Henry G. Adams

The one-room schoolhouse was now a ramshackled piece of the past, with its roof and floor caving in with age and neglect and the schoolyard choked with weeds. As I stopped to gaze on the old relic, my mind was flooded with memories, as if ghosts of the past were floating out through the broken panes of glass and were taking possession of my mind.

I recalled the days of my youth at this school, and suddenly I remembered Percival McFaith, an old neighbor whose farm I passed each day as a boy, telling me that he had attended this school. His exact words were: "That's where I learned my three R's—Readin', Rightin', and 'Rithmetic."

From the stories related to me by Percival, I learned that most of the boys in his era only attended school for a few years before they went off to work for their families. Girls always had the opportunity to stay in school longer, although most never went past the eighth grade.

Times were hard then and supplies were short. The few books were shared, and most students used slate boards instead of the pens, pencils, and paper tablets that I took for granted. Blackboard and chalk were available, and one of the worst punishments was writing that thing which you wouldn't do ever again on the board a hundred or so times. The leather strap was saved for major punishments, and my hands had felt its bite many times, as had Percival's before me.

As I gazed in through the broken panes of glass, I noticed the corner in which you stood wearing a dunce cap when you came to school without your homework or acted the class clown.

The potbelly stove which still stood in the center of the room was covered with cobwebs. The oldest boy had the responsibility of being first to school in the morning to make sure that the fire was going by the time the teacher and the other students arrived. The room would be so cold that all the desks would be circled around the stove in the morning, only to be pushed to the far walls in the afternoon as the stove's production exceeded demand. I could almost smell the scorching odor of drying mittens or coats which had been placed too close to the stove.

The desks were still there and bore the carved initials of many generations. If turned over, I suspect that hidden wads of chewing gum would still be found on the bottom of almost every seat.

The trophy case in the far corner had been smashed by vandals, and the trophies for the most flowers brought in and for the most birds sighted by a student each year were missing. The flower trophy was the most prestigious because the flower were seen by everyone, whereas the bird trophy was on the honor system. From the competition for these trophies grew the knowledge of and love of flowers and birds which I still have in my older age. Most students today would have difficulty distinguishing between a jack-in-the-pulpit and a cardinal.

My last glance inside the classroom was at the medicine cabinet on the back wall. I remember the many times that the teacher doubled as a nurse to patch up scratches and cuts acquired from climbing trees or from fistfights. The medicine cabinet also once contained a large brown bottle of cod-liver oil, which the teacher administered each day by the tablespoonful, followed with a piece of orange to kill the aftertaste. The students were overjoyed when the brown bottle was replaced with capsules which could be swallowed. Only the brave and the stupid bit into the capsules. With a bitter taste in my mouth, I turned from the window.

I walked to the cracked front steps of the school. The entryway where we hung our coats and left our overshoes was still standing. This entryway was the cause of my first strapping. We had a snowball fight outside, and one of the enemy ran to the entryway for protection. It was against the rules to throw snowballs into the entryway. The boy who was my intended victim kept sticking his head out, calling me names, and pulling his head back in. I saw movement, timed my throw, and let a snowball rip as hard as I could throw it. It landed with a loud splat! alongside my teacher's head. . . .

Turning, I walked through a grove of old maples on my way back to the car. The huge tree trunks still showed the carved hearts and initials of long-forgotten loves. One in particular brought back fond memories to me.

When we drove by the school the next day, I pointed it out to my son. In the very words of Percival McFaith, I said, "That's where I learned my three R's—Readin', Rightin', and 'Rithmetic."

He turned, grinned, and said, "Dad, you should have spent more time on your English and diction."

The Teacher Above

Lord, teach me to be
A child of Thy school,
That I may be tender
And kindly and true
To the highest profession
And calling and rule
Thou hast called any mortal
Humbly to do.
And help me, above all,
To carefully heed
My voice, my actions,
My method, my goal;
Remembering, I am the book
That they read,
And each of my scholars
Has a mind—and a soul.

D. L. Van Lanen

The School

EDNA JAQUES

At first, there was no school within fifteen miles of us. So dad thought that with four school-age kids running wild on the prairie, we must have a school. He drove to Moose Jaw and got in touch with the right people. I don't know how he did it, but one day we saw a wagon load of lumber arrive in the yard with four men riding on it. They were the carpenters who had come to build a school. Dad took them to the place where the school was to be built, about a mile from our place.

I do not remember who donated the little half-acre for the school and yard, but next day dad paced off the land (he was great at pacing land) and the foundations of the school were set down. I think the school was about twenty-by-forty—big enough to seat twenty kids. There were three windows on each side, a little platform at one end, a huge coal-burning stove at the back, and ten seats, two kids to a seat.

The first day there was great excitement for everyone. Just thirteen kids showed up: among them were our four (Clyde, Edna, Madge, Arlie); Wyatts, two girls and a little boy; Mary and Bob Banks and their cousin, Lou Jacobs; Fred Elliot, and I don't remember the names of the rest. We were a shy bunch of kids, playing on top of a little pile of lumber, stealing glances at each other—suddenly shy at meeting for the first time.

We all walked to school, of course, carrying our lunches in shiny new lard pails; lunches usually consisted of a couple of slices of good homemade bread, hard-boiled eggs, and if we were lucky, a couple of cookies.

61

The interior of a one-room school in Jaffrey, New Hampshire. Photo copyright William H. Johnson, Johnson's Photography (33093-00601).

Box Socials

Jerry Apps

No man is an island, entire of it self;

every man is a piece of the continent,

a part of the main. —John Donne

Country schools were much more than buildings where farm kids learned to read, write, and work with numbers. They were the center of their community, defining the geographic boundaries for the people who lived in the school district. In my home community, people knew they were part of the Chain O' Lake School District, just as those who lived south of us knew they were in Willow Grove, those to the west were in the Oasis district and so on.

Many wedding receptions, birthday celebrations, and anniversaries were held at the school. When soldiers returned from duty, a welcome home party was held there. When I completed army basic training and was on leave, the community turned out to see my pictures and learn about my adventures at Fort Eustis, Virginia, a far distant place to most of the people in our central Wisconsin school district.

The school was the social center for the entire community. I recall the receptions and parties held at my school when I was growing up. Three farmers played musical instruments. Frank Kolka played the concertina, Pinky (I never new his real first name) Eserhut strummed a banjo, and Harry Banks sawed on a fiddle. What wonderful music they made. . . .

Country schools were always short of money. There were never enough library books, maps, reference books, and the like. Not different from today, school boards were always stingy with money because they knew that it was their neighbors, through taxes, who were footing the bill.

Teachers constantly searched for ways to raise additional money. The box social was one way and besides, it was a splendid way to bring the community together for an evening of fun and good dining. At a box social the older school girls and the women in the community prepared a box lunch packed in a shoe box, oatmeal box, or other container about that size. The box was then wrapped as attractively as possible and brought to the school. An auctioneer sold them to the boy or man prepared to bid the highest amount. The person who fixed the box lunch then ate with the person who

62

bought it. All sales brought money to the school.

Of course many asides occurred. A young lady who wanted to make sure a favorite boy friend would buy her box lunch would describe it to the young man ahead of time. Unfortunately, when the other young men saw one of their friends bidding on only one box, they began bidding on this box too, making sure the young man paid dearly for the right to sit with his girl friend and taste her cooking.

Phoebe Bakken attended a one-room school, starting in 1927. She remembered a particular box social she attended. "I remember one guy who was auctioning and made a big mistake. He held up a nicely decorated box and said it must be a good one because it was nice and heavy. Every woman there knew that if you had a cake in it, it shouldn't be heavy. Cakes should be light and fluffy. He pulled a boner there."

Doris Lund, Rhinelander, remembered a box social when she was a country school student. "When we kids were in the country schools of Sugar Camp, we had get-togethers of all schools for certain events. At about ten years of age, I had my first school 'crush' on a young man who attended the Kathan Lake School. The school sponsored a box social. Dad and Mom decided to go, and I excitedly planned to take a box, too, hoping the 'right' person would buy it.

"After decorating a cardboard box (usually a round large-sized oatmeal box), Mom would bake some of her big sweet buns for the box. Sometimes she would fry chicken. But other times she would buy minced ham at Mangerson's store in Rhinelander. To me that was a real treat and cold cuts today cannot match it for flavor. With fresh produce from the garden tucked in and topped off with a home baked pie or cake, any man was well rewarded for his purchase price.

"I don't remember what I put in my box, but I expect Mom helped me with it. I do recall it was prettily trimmed with crepe paper flowers

Old schoolhouse in Granite, Oregon. Photo copyright Steve Terrill (OR-7-7-950).

and 'he' did buy it. But after all that preparation and anticipation, can you imagine I was too bashful to eat with him? That young man got his money's worth, since each box contained enough food for two."

Hazel Udelhoven taught more than sixteen years in Grant County country schools. She remembers a box social where somehow the young men found out which decorated box belonged to the teacher. The competitive bidding began with one thought in mind: buy the teacher's box and see what goodies are inside for lunch, at whatever cost. This was during the depression years, but even so the box brought more than twenty-five dollars, a lot of money in those days, particularly when the final bid on most boxes was between five and seven dollars.

The First Church

Edna Jaques

Grandpa and Grandma Jaques were dyed-in-the-wool Methodists, real oldtimers who believed in hell-fire and the wiles of the Devil and all his tribe. They went sedately to church every Sunday morning, with their bit of collection tied in the corner of grandma's handkerchief, for fear grandad might lose it. They never swore, or told a lie, or did a dishonest thing in all their sober lives, as far as I know. They were Christians, simple and honest and with a fear of hell-fire in their hearts.

So when we got settled in our first prairie house and a few neighbors came in, dad said we had better get a church started one way or the other. He started to hunt for a minister or missionary and found one in Rouleau, twelve miles east of us, by the name of Mr. Bard. I don't know what his first name was, but dad badgered him, and likely the church board in Rouleau, to have him come out and hold a little meeting in our house, for a start.

Then dad went around the little new settlement on horseback to tell the people about it. And so the minister came, driving a wild-eyed bronco hitched to a buggy across the trackless prairie with no road or landmarks of any kind, just a faint trail across the flats. The poor young fellow and the empty world he had come to, how frightened he must have been.

But he came. My mother would put down a couple of homemade mats on the floor that she carefully kept in a trunk under the stairs; she arranged a nice clean cloth on the top of the sewing machine, which he used for a pulpit. As I remember back, there was a sense of love and goodwill among us that was to last as long as they lived.

We three little girls sat on the bottom step of the stairs—no chairs for us. I remember Mr. Gallaugher (the first homesteader after us). I can see him sitting in dad's armchair in front of the stove, holding his little boy on his lap, and trying to make him sit still while the sermon was on.

After about two years of this they got a little school started and services were held there. Everyone came: Methodists, Presbyterians, Catholics, Anglicans—all so glad to be able to get out and talk to someone, just anyone who would listen; they would show off their babies, patting the little ones on the head, exchanging bits of news from home—just glad to meet and laugh; then, people would go home in their wagons. . . .

Fifty years, and yet my heart remembers the first church held in the country and in our homestead house, using the top of the sewing machine for a pulpit.

The Tualatin Plains Presbyterian Church, also known as "The Old Scotch Church" in Washington County, Oregon. Photo copyright Steve Terrill (OR-7-10-2015).

Church Supper Fare

EDWARD HARRIS HETH

The only basis for real fellowship with God and man is to live out in the open with both. —ROY HESSION

Autumn also means that we will soon be driving through the chill, translucent evenings to church suppers. There have been the walloping strawberries drowned in cream on buttered biscuits at the springtime socials on the church lawn, and also the sandwich-and-salad-laden baskets of the church picnic in summer. And the fat, tender hot dogs dripping with sauerkraut and chopped beef sauce that the Christian Men's Club sells at the village ball games to raise money for a new altar. But none of these has the opulence of foods nor the special jocular warmth of the church supper.

Perhaps it is coming into the warm, crowded, brightly lighted church basement out of the cold evening: here is friendliness and sharing, the basement redolent of boiling coffee, the women bustling in the kitchen, the children slamming slatted chairs, the men occupied at the tables, eating largely in silence but with rapt brown smiles. In part too, it is the sense of revelry and release from the summer's hard work; this is a harvest festival, the tables heaped with prize vegetables and scarlet woodbine running like a river of fire among them—while over our heads are the sanctity and protection of the vacant church. And, of course, it is also the wealth of food, supplied by the women in a spirit of (usually) cheerful competition.

There will always be two ham loaves, prepared by two rivaling sisters-in-law, both tall and string-like, both watching their loaves with hawks' eyes to see which is eaten sooner. One loaf is tart and somewhat exotically seasoned with curry and nutmeg, the other is studded with mushrooms and almonds. Both are richly pink, and each has a large boat of sauce beside it; but even on the sauces the sisters-in-law cannot agree. One pours the sauce over the ham loaf while it is baking, the other cooks hers separately. They stand like priestesses over their huge platters, on each of which are three or four miraculous loaves. Irene, once your plate has been heaped from her platter, will generously but dourly tell you that you must try some of Ethel's loaf too ("it's really quite good . . .") and Ethel, just as dourly but generously, will fill your plate from her platter until there's no room left for a peppercorn and then tell you to try just a sliver of Irene's ("it's lovely if you like funny spices"). Both platters, however, seem always to be emptied simultaneously, so the sisters-in-law remain good companions for another year—until a week or two before the next church supper, when their glances toward each other again grow apprehensive.

There'll be olives of all kinds, celery curls, carrot sticks, pickles, and preserves and gherkins and corn relish, hot rolls, and coleslaw, served warm as it should be. The children will be throwing coconut cupcakes at each other, until the pastor comes in, blinking and nodding all around cheerfully, not at all grave as he is on Sunday mornings after church in the vestibule. Our pastor, knowing the bent of the ham-loaf sisters-in-law, wisely if not charitably steers clear of the danger of having his plate heaped until there is room for nothing else and heads first toward the casserole over which Mrs. Dolly presides—his favorite.

The casseroles are at one end of the serving table, under the old print of "The Angelus." Among them will be macaroni; what Mrs. Emlyn mysteriously calls her "chop suey"; and, in a rather small baking dish, Mrs. Dolly's potato pudding.

One leaves the church basement with a sigh. There are free movies or community singing going on now, accompanied by the peaceful clatter of the Ladies' Aid doing dishes in the steamy kitchen. On lucky years, as you step from the noisy basement into the quiet night, the year's first snowfall will have begun.

Country church in the middle of a field in Nebraska. Photo copyright Jessie Walker, Jessie Walker Associates (00054-01707.0037).

67

Baking Powder Biscuits

Makes 8 servings

2 cups all-purpose flour	1 tablespoon sugar
½ teaspoon salt	½ cup vegetable shortening
4 teaspoons baking powder	⅔ cup milk
½ teaspoon cream of tartar	

In a large bowl, sift together flour, salt, baking powder, cream of tartar, and sugar. Cut in shortening until mixture is the consistency of coarse crumbs. Add milk all at once; stir just until dough forms a ball around a fork. Turn dough onto lightly floured surface; knead 30 seconds. Pat into a circle that is ⅔-inch-thick. Use a 2-inch biscuit cutter to cut into rounds.

A Church-Style Supper

Biscuit-Topped Chicken Pie

Makes 6 servings

4 cups cooked chicken	½ teaspoon black pepper
6 tablespoons butter	Salt
6 tablespoons all-purpose flour	12 small white onions, cooked
2 cups chicken broth	¾ cup peas, cooked and drained
1 cup heavy cream	

Preheat oven to 450° F. Arrange chicken in 2-quart casserole or deep-dish pie plate; set aside. In a medium saucepan, melt butter. Whisk in flour; cook over low heat, whisking constantly, for 2 minutes without browning flour. Slowly stir in broth, cream, pepper, and salt to taste. Cook and stir over medium heat, or until thickened and smooth. Remove from heat and gently stir in cooked onions and peas. Pour sauce over chicken. Prepare Baking Powder Biscuits. Place biscuits on top, with edges touching. Bake for 10 to 15minutes, or until biscuits are golden.

COUNTRY COCONUT CAKE

Makes 12 servings

3 cups all-purpose flour	¾ cup butter, cut up in small pieces
1 tablespoon baking powder	1 cup milk
¼ teaspoon salt	1 tablespoon vanilla
1½ cups granulated sugar	Shredded coconut
4 large eggs	

At least two hours in advance, prepare WHIPPED CREAM FILLING; refrigerate until ready to use. Preheat oven to 350° F. Grease three 9-inch round cake pans. Line bottoms with waxed paper; grease the waxed paper. Dust bottoms and sides lightly with flour; tap out excess. In a large bowl, sift together flour, baking powder, and salt; set aside. In a large bowl, combine sugar and eggs; beat at medium speed of electric mixer for 1 minute, or until lemon-colored. Beat in butter, a little at a time, along with milk and vanilla. Beat for 2 minutes. Reduce speed to low. Gradually add flour mixture, beating well after each addition. Beat for 1 minute. Divide batter evenly among prepared pans. Bake for 20 minutes, or until a wooden pick inserted in the center comes out clean. Remove from oven. Cool in pans on wire racks for 20 minutes. Gently turn layers out onto racks. Remove waxed paper from layers. Cool completely.

While cake is cooling, prepare CREAM CHEESE FROSTING. To assemble cake, place one cake layer on large cake platter. Spread with half of the WHIPPED CREAM FILLING. Top with second cake layer. Spread with remaining WHIPPED CREAM FILLING. Place remaining layer on top. Spread CREAM CHEESE FROSTING over sides and top of cake. Sprinkle top with additional shredded coconut.

CREAM CHEESE FROSTING

6	ounces cream cheese
½	cup butter, softened
¼	teaspoon salt
1	pound powdered sugar
3	tablespoons milk
1	tablespoon extract

In small bowl, combine cream cheese and butter; beat on medium speed until smooth. Add salt, powdered sugar, milk, and vanilla; blend until smooth.

WHIPPED CREAM FILLING

1	tablespoon cornstarch
1	tablespoon milk
1¼	cups heavy cream
¾	cup granulated sugar
2	tablespoons coconut milk
½	cup unsalted butter, softened
1	cup shredded coconut

In a small bowl, dissolve cornstarch in milk; set aside. In a heavy saucepan, combine cream, granulated sugar, and coconut milk. Bring to a simmer over medium heat. Stir cornstarch mixture into cream mixture; cook and stir 3 minutes, or until slightly thickened. Add butter and coconut; cook and stir 3 minutes. Remove from heat; cool to room temperature. Refrigerate for at least 2 hours, or until thickened.

Surprise Parties

EDNA JAQUES

As long as you notice, and have to count the steps, you are not yet dancing but only learning to dance. —C. S. LEWIS

In the early years, nearly all of the homesteaders were young married couples with one or two children; in the wintertime when there was little work to do they would get bored to death. Then someone would plan a surprise party, go on horseback around the neighborhood and tell everyone to come to a party at someone's house, usually ours, as my mother loved company and was a good entertainer and most important we had a piano. Not that they needed entertaining; just being together to talk and listen was enough to make them happy.

Because dad was the oldest family man in the settlement (he was just thirty-seven), it usually fell to our lot to be the place where the party was held; and we all liked surprises.

As a rule they would meet at someone's house and all come together in a big sleigh, drive quietly into the yard and then all at once let out a war whoop that would deafen a horse; amid laughter and hellos they would pile into the house and start to have fun.

After the horses were put in the barn, the men would come into the house and start to throw out the furniture, all except the stove, and the way would be cleared for a good old square dance. Someone would run over to grandad's and get them to come over. Grandpa would bring his fiddle (that his family had brought from the old country a hundred years before), and he would perch himself on a stool in the corner of the room, start to saw away, and the dance was on. . . .

There was no classical slow dance music for him; he played all the old favorites by ear: "Turkey in the Straw," "Irish Wash Woman," "Money Musk," "Comin' Through the Rye." How they all danced in that tiny room, I do not know. But the fun went on as they bumped into each other, laughing; dipping and swaying and kicking up their heels, they would stop to pant and get a drink of water, and start again.

The babies would have been put away upstairs on the bed, and younger ones would sit on the stairs with us; I don't know who enjoyed it the most, the dancers or the spectators.

Around midnight, the coffee pot would be put on and the lunches unpacked (that they had brought). Salmon sandwiches were the favorite, along with angel cakes and cookies. There was never any drinking; my mother would have scalped anyone who dared bring a bottle or a deck of cards into the house; they were the Devil's tools, she would say.

After lunch the babies would be brought downstairs, rosy and smiling, and the older children would be wrapped up to their very eyes, and the party was over.

Then they would all join hands making a circle in the little room and sing, "Should auld acquaintance be forgot, and never brought to mind . . . ," grandad playing it on his violin and all the people singing.

Then we would stand outside and watch them go, hearing the sleigh bells getting fainter and fainter, falling into the eternal silence that even to this day hangs above the lonely prairie giving an eerie feeling, as if the earth had just been finished and was still half-asleep.

The winter of 1906-07 was one of the coldest and snowiest winters ever recorded in Saskatchewan. The first blizzard came about the middle of October, and it hardly let up day or night until spring. But one day it eased off a bit, and what did we see coming along the trail from the west but a sleigh with a team of horses and two young men in it.

They drove into the yard, and my father and brothers went out, and before they could say they couldn't stay, my father had the horses in the barn, and we had them in the house, and my mother was getting a meal on the table. Before we finished eating, a beautiful blizzard had come up and kept them there for three days and nights.

They were good singers and good talkers—how we enjoyed them; just to hear a different voice raised in laughter was balm to our lonely hearts. I don't think we ever stopped laughing and singing and telling stories.

When the storm stopped the third day, they hitched up and went on their way, and we never saw them again; but my sister and I have loved them all our lives.

The Reapers Come

Singing, the reapers homeward come, Io! Io!
Merrily singing the harvest home, Io! Io!
Along the field, along the road,
Where autumn is scattering leaves abroad,
Homeward cometh the ripe last load, Io! Io!

Singers are filling the twilight dim
With the cheerful song, Io! Io!
The spirit of song ascends to Him
Who causeth the corn to grow.
He freely sent the gentle rain,
The summer sun glorified hill and plain,
To golden perfection brought the grain, Io! Io!

Silently, nightly, fell the dew,
Gently the rain, Io! Io!
But who can tell how the green corn grew,
Or who beheld it grow?
Oh! God the good, in sun and rain,
He look'd on the flourishing fields and grain,
Till they all appear'd on hill and plain
Like living gold, Io! Io!

AUTHOR UNKNOWN

Chapter Four

COUNTRY FAMILY, FRIENDS, AND NEIGHBORS

Short Days and Yellow Lamplight

BEN LOGAN

Home joys are the most delightful earth affords, and the joy of parents in their children is the most holy joy of humanity. —J. H. PESTALOZZI

When Mother decided to use the evening for baking, the smell of new bread filled the house. One by one, we would slip out until the dining room was deserted and we were all gathered around the kitchen stove, eating slices of hot bread.

If it weren't bread, it had to be some other kind of food. We were always starving by the middle of the evening. We'd shell little ears of popcorn, and the popping sound and smell of hot butter in the kitchen would bring faces peeking around from the dining room. We'd go to the cellar for apples, or make fudge, first cracking hickory nuts, the dry shells flying around the room like bullets. Sometimes we even tried making taffy, pulling the long loops until the candy was almost white, getting it stuck on ourselves and, once, all over the dog.

For some reason food made us think about playing cards, and the two ideas didn't mix, or, rather, mixed all too well. When the cards got too sticky to shuffle, we went to something else. Laurance was lost in a pile of bee magazines. Junior was always fixing something—a clock, a part off the car—so that we got used to springs flying at us and screws rolling around the table. Lee might be studying the taxidermy course that was going to make him a fortune. He had already mounted one scrawny squirrel. Lyle said it reminded him of the year there weren't any acorns.

Nothing very exciting or unusual happened on winter evenings like those. The seven of us just gathered in a close and quiet warmth, feeling secure and immensely pleased with ourselves when we said good night and went off to our cold beds. Such evenings were more fragile than we knew.

Once Father brought home a new lamp for the dining-room table, an Aladdin with a cone-shaped mantle. The light it gave was white, like the light from a bare electric bulb in a

74

store. The new lamp gave more light, opening up the corners of the dining room, letting us scatter away from the little circle we'd always formed around the old Rayo.

I remember Mother standing in the doorway to the kitchen one night, frowning in at us. "I'm not sure I like that new lamp."

Father was at his usual place at the table. "Why not? Burns less kerosene."

"Look where everyone is."

We were scattered. There was even enough light to read by on the far side of the stove.

"We're all here," Father said.

"Not like we used to be."

Father looked at the empty chairs around the table. "Want to go back to the old lamp?"

"I don't think it's the lamp. I think it's us. Does a new lamp have to change where we sit at night?"

Father's eyes found us, one by one. Then he made a little motion with his head. We came out of our corners and slid into our old places at the table, smiling at each other, a little embarrassed to be hearing this talk.

Mother sat down with us and nodded. "That's better."

Large country kitchen with wood stove and bright red, yellow, and blue spatterware displayed. Photo copyright Jessie Walker and Associates (00021-2100.0002).

COUNTRY FAMILY, FRIENDS, AND NEIGHBORS

Country Visiting

MARY MARGARET MCBRIDE

Country visiting usually meant spending the day and once in a while the night. Some pretty fall morning when I was sweeping the front porch, I'd spy, say, the Johnsons' surrey driving up the dusty road toward our house. Mr. Johnson and his wife would be in the front seat and squashed in between them would be the baby. . . . In the back seat would be Sue, my age, and her older sister, Lucille, and trailing along behind, Harry on horseback.

"Get out, get out," my father would shout hospitably, as the surrey drew up in front of the hitching block. I would run to tell Mama and she, drying her hands on her apron, would rush to the smokehouse for a few slices of ham or to the backyard to catch a couple of pullets for company dinner.

Glad as we all were to see the Johnsons we knew that the visit was not entirely social. Menfolks on a farm were too busy to take much time out for visiting unless business was afoot. Maybe Mr. Johnson wanted to borrow our plow or cultivator for a few days. Or perhaps it was a trading proposition. That horse ambling up our lane with Harry on his back may have been brought along to exchange for one of our mules. Lots of men came to our house to barter, for Papa was known to the whole county as a great trader. His joy in thinking he had gotten the better of the deal was always touching. Sometimes he really did win. But once in a while it turned out that his fine bargain had the blind staggers or was splay-footed.

There weren't many real parties in the country except, once in a while, a church supper or strawberry festival, with Japanese lanterns in the trees and plank tables covered with Mama's and other women's best white tablecloths. Wild roses and honeysuckle growing all over the churchyard furnished the decorations and the perfume, too. You could take your choice of strawberry short-cake made with very short biscuit dough, smothered with butter while hot and then drowned in strawberries, strawberry ice cream, or just plain strawberries and cream. This kind of entertainment was so simple and infrequent that when we moved to town the gaiety at first quite dazzled me.

Cows graze in a pasture rimmed by autumn-colored trees in Forest County, Wisconsin. Photo copyright by Darryl Beers (MT-01J89-17).

When Company Comes

June Masters Bacher

Fish and visitors smell in three days. —Benjamin Franklin

The old red rooster had been crowing all day—a sure sign of company. The children imitated his loud predictions and flapped their arms in glee. Great-grandmother with equal anticipation set to work at the old "Home Comfort" range, chanting as she baked: "My nose itches; I smell peaches; somebody's comin' with a hole in his breeches!

Between the rooster's crows and Granny's nose there could be no mistake. There could be, and was, a mistake in identity, however. The "breeches" line indicated arrival of a gentleman—probably a seldom drummer or the circuit rider. Wrong! When the stage rattled up to Covey's Corner, it delivered a letter from Cousin Lola saying that she would arrive in mid-August. It was mid-August. So it delivered Cousin Lola as well.

Cousin Lola, who was not a relative, really, but a very dear friend of my great-grandmother's, came from "Back East," had "lived abroad," once had a count kiss the tips of her fingers, and always smelled of verbenas. (This was how my grandmother, who was a little girl at the time, described her.) Cousin Lola was also responsible for the chapter in my great-grandmother's cookbook entitled, "Small Points on Table Etiquette." It was her plan to "marry royalty" and so her study on behavior at the dining table was quite complete. Great-grandmother took a healthy interest in food, for royalty or otherwise; so as Cousin Lola fanned herself and chatted fervently, her friend took copious notes. Though some of the outdated ideas are like the odors of an old unaired closet, in such aroma are memories stored.

"Delicacy of manner at table stamps both man and woman for one can discern, at a glance, whether a person has proper training for eating well," Cousin Lola dictated knowingly. What follows are the "small points" as recorded by Great-Gran.

Hold the knife and fork properly . . . eat without the slightest smack . . . drink without a gargle . . . use the napkin rightly . . . make no unseemly noise with the implements, and last but not least, eat slowly (with the mouth closed except to feed it) . . . masticate thoroughly.

Don't, when you drink, elevate your glass as if you were going to stand it inverted on the nose. Bring the glass perpendicularly to the lips, and then lift it to a slight angle. Never, never drain the glass. Drink sparingly and do so gently—not pouring the contents down the throat like water turned out of a pitcher.

When seating yourself at the table, unfold your napkin and lay it across your lap in such a manner that it cannot slide to the floor. A gentleman should place it across his right knee, never the left. Do not tuck it into your neck like a child's bib. For an old person, however, it is well to attach the napkin to a napkin hook and slip it into the vest or dress buttonholes or sew a broad tape at two places on the napkin and pass it over the head.

Finger bowls are as needful as the napkin. They should be half filled with water with a leaf or two of sweet verbena, an orange blossom, or a slice of lemon to wipe the fingers on. The fingertips are slightly dipped into the bowl, the nectar squeezed on, then they are dried softly upon the napkin.

Ladies have frequently an affected way of holding the knife halfway down its length, as if it were too big for their little hands; but this is weak; and the knife should be grasped freely by the handle, the forefinger being the only one to touch the blade at its root. At the conclusion, the knife and fork must be laid side by side across the middle of the plate—*never* crossed.

One's teeth are not to be picked at the table; but if it is impossible to hinder, it must take place behind the napkin. To pick one's teeth, suck on a corn cob, or gnaw on a bone gives a lady the look of caring a little too much for the pleasures of the table. And on no account is one to suck the fingers afterwards.

All these points should be most carefully taught to children, and then they will always feel at their ease at the grandest tables in the land. There is no position where the innate refinement of a person is more fully exhibited than at the table, and nowhere that those who have not been trained in table etiquette feel more keenly their deficiencies. The knife should never transport food to the mouth. The knife can be used to cut the pieces of meat finely as large pieces are indelicate. Be careful to keep the mouth quiet. It is the opening of the lips which causes the smacking that is disgusting. At grand tables, several knives and forks are placed, knives at the right of the plate, forks at the left. The small ones for game and dessert are tucked under the edges of the plate; the large ones for the main course are placed on the outside. None of these must be clattered when used. When passing the plate for second helpings, lay them together on the plate noiselessly.

Soup must always be served as a first course. Sip it from the sides of dessert spoons; do not suck audibly from the ends. Never ask for seconds. If the hostess asks you to take a second plate, you must politely decline. Fish chowder is the only exception.

If, to conclude, one seats one's self properly at the table and takes reason into account, one is apt to do tolerably well. One must not pull one's chair too closely to the table; and arms must lie completely against one's body. Nor is one to ever touch any of the dishes.

At the end of the chapter there is a section cut from a letter dated 1894: "I am sending you some of my ways of laying the table for polite society dinners." A second clipping (dated the same year) reads: "Here are the 'French Words in Cooking' you asked for . . ." and it includes a list from *aspic* to *vol au vents*. The postmark is faded with time, but the excerpts lead us of the fourth generation to suppose Cousin Lola married a Frenchman. Great-grandmother penned, "Lola married well," and then, as was her style, she clinched it with an adage: "Where there's a will, there's a way."

Rural Mail

That winter roared in late and cold,
The phone line twisted down.
Snow covered every fence and road
And piled high all around.
We had a good-sized "tater" bin,
Some flour, meal, and grits,
With cans of lard and smokehouse meats
So we made the best of it.
No mail came in, none went out,
The phone was dead and so
We starved for news: Few folks had
"Newfangled" radios.
It seemed an age before the drifts
Packed down to hold a sleigh
And the mailman's driving horse, shar-shod,
Came jingling out our way.
We'd scooped a path down to the box,
His eggshell sleigh turned in,
The horse was warm and blowing some

He shouted "Hi" and grinned.
Mail-order packages piled high,
Seed catalogues, and bills
About somebody's auction sale
Away back in the hills.

Mom took most of the letters
And handed Pa the rest.
The seed books went to Grandpa
But, oh, the very best
That spring and summer catalogue
Square-cut and thick, it seemed,
Shall ever be the center of
A thousand winter dreams.
That sweet fresh ink aroma
Until this day prevails:
I wish I were a kid again
Waiting for the rural mail!

D. A. HOOVER

COUNTRY FRIENDS

Through all the pleasant meadow-side
The grass grew shoulder high,
Till the shining scythes went far and wide
And cut it down to dry.
Oh, what a joy to clamber there,
Oh, what a place for play,
With the sweet, the dim, the dusty air,
The happy hills of hay!

ROBERT LOUIS STEVENSON

The Pasture

I'm going out to clean the pasture spring;
I'll only stop to rake the leaves away
(And wait to watch the water clear, I may):
I sha'n't be gone long.—You come too.

I'm going out to fetch the little calf
That's standing by the mother. It's so young,
It totters when she licks it with her tongue.
I sha'n't be gone long.—You come too.

ROBERT FROST

Friendship depends not upon fancy, imagination or sentiment, but upon character. There is no man so poor that he is not rich if he has a friend; there is no man so rich that he is not poor without a friend.

AUTHOR UNKNOWN

Strawberry Jam

I went visiting Miss Melinda,
    Miss Melinda Brown.
She has a cottage out in the country;
    I live here in town.

"Guess what I've got for your dinner, dearie,"
    Miss Melinda said.
"Strawberry jam," for my nose had guessed it!
    "Strawberry jam and bread."

Strawberry jam in the corner cupboard,
    On the middle shelf.
She let me stand on a chair and tiptoe,
    Get it down myself.

Somehow, visiting Miss Melinda,
    Time goes by on wings.
"What do you do all alone," I ask her.
    "I make jam and things."

When it was time to go home I kissed her.
    "Thanks for the lovely day!"
"Thank you for coming," said Miss Melinda,
    "Come again right away!"

MAY JUSTUS

My Neighbor

All my neighbor did was wave
    from his field across the way,
But his warm and kindly gesture
    was the highlight of my day!

In that golden moment
    There was a blending of our hearts,
A mood of rapturous joy
    That only friendship can impart.

JOY BELLE BURGESS

O Home-Folks!

O Home-Folks! you're the best of all
"At ranges this terreschul ball,—
But, north er south, er east er west,
It's home where you're at your best.—

It's home—it's home your faces shine,
In-nunder your own fig and vine—
Your fambly and your neighbors 'bout
Ye, and the latch-string hangin' out.

Home-Folks—*at home*,—I know o' one
Old feller now 'at hain't got none.—
Invite him—he may hold back some—
But *you* invite him, and he'll come.

JAMES WHITCOMB RILEY

The Country Store

EVAN JONES

If the world seems cold to you, kindle fires to warm it. —AUTHOR UNKNOWN

People who grew up outside large cities, as he had, Dwight Eisenhower once said, had priceless memories that "so often centered around the retail store, the open cracker barrel . . . Places where things were sold and people gathered . . . They were the social centers of our time. . . ."

A singularly American institution, the country store flourished in and took its character from the nineteenth century. It isn't simply fond memory that makes such stores the small town centers of the past. In hundreds of instances the merchant who built a crossroads emporium was the founder of a hamlet that grew into a town. As much as the country doctor, the country storekeeper was a lifeline—farmers and townspeople depended upon him for hardware, groceries, drugs, dry goods, feed for livestock and seed to grow crops.

Often he was also the postmaster, and his store, as President Eisenhower remembered, was the gathering place that mattered. Here, according to one historian, "politics, religion, and neighbors were discussed . . . important government matters were ultimately settled. Certainly statesmen had to reckon with . . . public opinion generated and cultivated around the stove of the country store."

The cracker-barrel philosopher earned his manhood in the village store's inner circle; here the potbellied glow drew winter loungers to rickety chairs and one hospitable barrel was open to cracker munchers all year round while another served as a table on which checkers could be played. The philosophy was a blend of homilies from the weather-wise, tall stories from those who might have gone to sea or come home from war, and shrewd arguments about almost any subject, political or general. Cracker-barrel wit came as close to entertaining the country people of the nineteenth century as have radio and television in the twentieth.

Today, however, the revival of the country store is based not so much on its social implications as on the merchandising concept that a good rural commissary, particularly in an age of specialization, can be a retail oasis. Tainted by opportunism as it seems in too many instances, that revival had its beginnings when three country stores were preserved as museums and opened to the public shortly before World War II. But the idea of bringing back old-time mercantilism as a contemporary business belongs to Vrest Orton, the plain-spoken Yankee whose father and grandfather had been the village merchants in North Calais, Vermont.

Orton himself first worked in that country store at the age of ten when he was charged with trimming and filling the huge brass kerosene lamps. By the time he had put college behind him, he was launched on a literary career that established him as a bibliophile and New York magazine writer and editor whose nostalgia for New England caused him to buy a country home in Weston, on the edge of Green Mountain National Forest. Almost instinctively, he became a preservationist.

In the 1930s he joined Weston friends in a volunteer effort to restore the village to its once simple architectural beauty. "It was a labor of love," Orton says today. As Weston was relieved of its run-down look, Orton helped to establish a guild of craftsmen to preserve the manual skills of yesterday. "We had classes and taught people how to do things properly—things like quilting and metalwork, woodwork—the way their grandparents had done them. But then the war came, and we had other things to do."

Not until the fall of 1945 was Orton able to seriously pursue the dream that urged him to revive what he described as "an authentic, old-fashioned, rural operating store, as near as possible to the northern Vermont store my father had run." On a return trip to the village of his boyhood, he discovered that trees and bushes obscured the site of the disintegrated North Calais emporium, but that some of the fixtures had gone to neighboring storekeepers who were willing to sell them. And, as luck would have it, he found a collection of the glass negatives of a local photographer that included pictures of the old frame building of "Teachout & Orton."

"The whole thing comes down to this,"

Orton said one day in 1975. "We've lost track of the fact that the purpose of life is personal achievement." Having set his sights on achieving a restoration of the family store, he moved the fixtures he had found in 1945 to Weston and, consulting the old photographs, proved to his satisfaction that a century-old main street building was almost identical to the one that had vanished from North Calais. It had been built in 1828 as a country inn, and it was two and a half stories tall "with the same gable-end facade of my father's place" and the same sort of double-decked porch across the front.

From the posts of that porch, when the time came, he hung a gold-leafed sign: "The Vermont Country Store." A giant, cylindrical 1870-style black iron stove was moved into the center of the first floor, and around that, Orton remembers, he fashioned the interior with salvaged fixtures in an effort to reproduce the atmosphere that would make any cracker-barrel philosopher completely at home. To stock shelves and counters he determined to bring back "useful, sensible, practical things that had been common in American homes fifty years ago," and he sought out small New England manufacturers and persuaded them to supply the new venture. "I had the idea there were such things as 'gourmet' housewares, long before other people began to overuse the word, and I looked for things that worked not just little gadgets."

His wife, Mary Ellen Orton, had a calico apron that had belonged to her grandmother, and they found a neighboring seamstress to reproduce it exactly; it proved to be a stroke that was soon followed by a mail-order market of housekeepers delighted to be able to buy so old-fashioned but serviceable an item. He installed equipment to turn out stone-ground flour and cornmeal more than a decade before "natural foods" became a nationwide enthusiasm. Other

83

COUNTRY FAMILY, FRIENDS, AND NEIGHBORS

New Englanders were induced to put up baked beans in cans in accordance with an Orton recipe—for he believed that all other commercially canned beans were steamed and therefore lacked Yankee authenticity.

"I want to save what's worth saving—which is different from going backwards," Vrest Orton said. "We gathered an increasing array of merchandise which was different from all other stores—and it also proved to be fascinating to customers who remembered the old days when things were made to use and to last."

The Country Store

I know city stores are very neat,
    in fact, I think they're fine,
With their new-fangled fixtures,
    and their clerks arrayed in line;
And with their bright new wares
    displayed so tidily about,
It tempts you much to purchase—
    of this there is no doubt.

Somehow you feel you're welcome
    in every country store;
They are never there too busy
    to talk life's problems o'er.
But custom ever changes;
    city business of today
Is strictly classed as business,
    and there's nothing else to say.

WILLIAM F. HUNT

Farmstand offering newly harvested apples and bittersweet in Deerfield, Massachusetts. Photo copyright William H. Johnson, Johnson's Photography (22202-00102).

The Huskers

It was late in mild October, and the long autumnal rain
Had left the summer harvest-fields all green with grass again;
The first sharp frosts had fallen, leaving all the woodlands gay
With the hues of summer's rainbow, or the meadow flowers of May.

Through a thin, dry mist, that morning, the sun rose broad and red,
At first a rayless disk of fire, he brightened as he sped;
Yet, even his noontide glory fell chastened and subdued,
On the cornfields and the orchards, and softly pictured wood.

And all that quiet afternoon, slow sloping to the night,
He wove with golden shuttle the haze with yellow light;
Slanting through the painted beeches, he glorified the hill;
And, beneath it, pond and meadow lay brighter, greener still.

And shouting boys in woodland haunts caught glimpses of that sky,
Flecked by the many-tinted leaves, and laughed, they knew not why;
And school-girls, gay with aster-flowers, beside the meadow brooks,
Mingled the glow of autumn with the sunshine of sweet looks.

From spire and barn looked westerly the patient weathercocks;
But even the birches on the hill stood motionless as rocks.
No sound was in the woodlands, save the squirrel's dropping shell,
And the yellow leaves among the boughs, low rustling as they fell.

The summer grains were harvested; the stubblefields lay dry,
Where June winds rolled, in light and shade, the pale green waves of rye;
But still, on gentle hill-slopes, in valleys fringed with wood,
Ungathered, bleaching in the sun, the heavy corn crop stood.

Bent low, by autumn's wind and rain, through husks that, dry and sere,
Unfolded from their ripened charge, shone out the yellow ear;
Beneath, the turnip lay concealed, in many a verdant fold,
And glistened in the slanting light the pumpkin's sphere of gold.

There wrought the busy harvesters; and many a creaking wain
Bore slowly to the long barn-floor is load of husk and grain;
Till broad and red, as when he rose, the sun sank down, at last,
And like a merry guest's farewell, the day in brightness passed.

JOHN GREENLEAF WHITTIER

Cornfields awaiting harvesting in early autumn in Hoosic, New York. Photo copyright William H. Johnson, Johnson's Photography (23303-00102).

87

The Mail's Here!

WILLIAM AND SARAH TURNBAUGH

*In proportion as our inward life fails,
we go more constantly and desperately
to the post office.* —HENRY DAVID THOREAU

In their selection of the family mailbox, as in their choice of President, Americans proved to be capricious and individualistic. Early receptacles for the mail very often consisted of any handy container that could be perched or posted at the end of a farm lane or along a country road. The Postmaster General reported in 1897 on the random array of boxes that typically presented itself to rural carriers, using a Washington state example: "The 'boxes' are of sundry shapes, sizes, and colors. One man has a lard pall hung out on a fence post; three or four have nailed up empty coal oil cans, and a few have utilized syrup cans. . . . Old apple boxes, soapboxes, cigar boxes, and in one instance a wagon box, adorn the entrances to farms all over the valley." Another rural carrier encountered a sign beside a crack in a fence, requesting him to "Put the Male Hear." As a matter of fact, this technique did have its historical precedents. Early explorers and gold-seekers crossing the Great Plains frequently left messages on a scrap of paper or hide clamped in a split twig or forked stick along the trail. But this was now the twentieth century, and the official U.S. Mail, transported between sender and receiver with great purposefulness (and at considerable expense), deserved—nay, demanded—a suitable depository at the completion of its journey.

The minimal expectation was that the receptacle would be placed conveniently at the side of the road at a height that would enable the carrier to execute his transactions from the seat of his buggy. Beyond that, individuality ruled. From time to time the Post Office Department tried various approaches to improve and standardize the mailboxes on rural delivery routes. Nearby farmers came to a small Indiana town in the spring of 1900 to pick up boxes supplied by the government at a cost of $2.60 each. But apparently not everyone elected to obtain one of the special devices, choosing instead to supply their own in accordance with whim and the availability of empty tins or crates. . . .

88

A typical . . . box . . .was invented and manufactured by William S. Isham of Maple Hill, Kansas. His sturdy metal box was designed for the convenience of a driver seated in a wagon. It was a horizontal cylinder, sealed at both ends, its front-opening flap hinged at the top. Not all boxes were quite so practical in their design. One contemporary advertiser expressed the view that many of this competitors' mailboxes were "better fitted for rat-traps. . . ."

In 1915, an engineer with the Department, Roy J. Joroleman, designed a tunnel-shaped metal box with a snap-close hinged front and movable flag. Joroleman's box looked to the future. It was well suited for use by rural carriers seated in automobiles, which were effectively replacing the horse-drawn buggy on

A snow-covered country lane lined with sugar maples in Hebron, New Hampshire. Photo copyright William H. Johnson, Johnson's Photography (23071-00105).

the long rural routes. Postmaster General Albert Burleson gave Joroleman's design his official endorsement, and boxes manufactured to those specifications by private companies were entitled to bear the designation "Approved by the Postmaster General." In 1928 the Department extended official sanction to a larger version of the box, designed to accommodate parcels. By far, the most common rural delivery boxes in use even today are of the "Approved" style.

Chapter Five

FESTIVALS, FAIRS, AND FUN

May Day

MARGARITA CUFF

Cherish all your happy moments:

they make a fine cushion for old age.

–CHRISTOPHER MORLEY

May Day has been left largely to the children. Though it was not part of the formal school program, the beautiful May pole dance was the highlight of the spring term in many schools. It was often presented by kindergarten classes. Viroqua's May Day program of 1916 was typical of these early Wisconsin celebrations.

Pretty Miss Edith Tainter, the kindergarten teacher, took her class on an excursion into the country to "gather in the May." They picked forsythia, dogwood, and wild plum, jack-in-the-pulpit, anemones, and hepatica. Blue, yellow, and white violets were brought back, too, to decorate the schoolrooms and grounds where the May Day festival would be held.

On May Day itself, all classes, including high school, were dismissed for the occasion, and everyone in town was invited to the program. Often May Day participants wore their Sunday best—frilly, white dresses for the girls and suits for the boys—but Miss Tainter had grander plans. The excited kindergarten girls were colorfully costumed as butterflies and flowers. The boys were dressed to represent grasshoppers in green suits with wings attached to their backs and caps with large, black eyes.

To open the program, the flowers did a graceful dance imitating a bud opening to full bloom. The girl who had been chosen Queen of the May was crowned with wreaths of wildflowers. Dressed in regal finery, she sat with her court in a lovely flower arbor. The path to her throne was lined with bouquets, and all activities centered around her. Near the queen's bower stood a gaily painted May pole. The pole was trimmed with wreaths of flowers and long colored ribbons fluttered from the top.

As the May dance began, each of the children grasped the end of a ribbon. Then, to music from an organ that had been moved outside for the event, they danced in and out around the pole, weaving over and under the other ribbons. The streamers were wound about the pole, then unwound, and finally rewound again. When the sprightly dancers had finished, the pole was covered from top to bottom with a beautiful coat of braided ribbons.

Viroqua's charming program was one of the last held there, and though some communities continued the practice longer, public May Day festivals were increasingly a thing of the past after World War I. For one thing, the program took a great deal of time to prepare, for the dances—especially the May pole dance—and pantomimes were rather intricate. May Day planners throughout the state were fraught with anxiety about the unpredictable weather, too. It could chill and dampen the spirits as well as the bodies of the young performers and their guests. Cold rains or even snow showers were not improbable, and May Day programs could no more be taken inside than a parade of surreys.

Yet some May Day festivities continued. People decorated homes and schools and banked church altars with bouquets of wildflowers. Picnics were held to celebrate the first day of May and the beginning of summer vacation. In the schools, children made tiny May baskets and filled them with delicate spring blossoms. The baskets were of various shapes, sizes, and colors, but they all had handles long enough to slip easily over doorknobs on the homes of neighbors and friends.

Anytime from dawn to dusk on the first day of May, children took their baskets and tiptoed to the front door of a friend's home. With much giggling and whispering, they hung a pretty basket of flowers over the knob, knocked on the door, and sprinted away to hide behind the nearest tree or clump of bushes. If the children were caught at this delightful prank, they received a kiss. Their laughing, squealing embarrassment at such a reward was usually short-lived as they ran off to deliver more of their May baskets.

Finally even schools abandoned the preparation of May baskets in their classes, leaving the custom of hanging floral gifts on friendly doors to individual families. During the last decade, the children's May Day visitations have declined drastically. Yet even today, a few children continue to make May baskets at home, filling them with dandelions, violets, cowslips, sprigs of pussy willows, even cookies, nuts, and small candies. May Day traditions are too full of meaning and too charming to die of neglect, so if there are youngsters in your family, celebrate May Day with them this spring.

MAKE A MAY BASKET

May baskets can be as plain or as frilly as you choose. For a really dainty one, weave a narrow ribbon through the top of a paper doily. Then pull the ribbon like a drawstring to form a cup. Line the cup with colored tissue paper, and tie on a ribbon for a handle.

Another style children like to make uses strips of construction paper cut in equal lengths (save one strip for a handle). Weave the strips together to make a mat. Then lift up the corners and fasten the sides with tape or glue. Attach the handle, and you're ready to fill the basket.

One of the easiest baskets is made by rolling pretty paper into a cone. You might even use white paper and let the children draw designs on it. Then simply paste or tape the seam and attach a handle.

You can also cover small cans (those for frozen juices work well) or cardboard boxes with flowered wallpaper or wrapping paper for quick and easy baskets, but remember to keep them small. Colored pipe cleaners make good handles.

To fill your baskets, you should start with fresh flowers if possible. Otherwise, you might include blossoms made of paper or ribbon, or strawflowers. Try adding a spring poem, gifts of

seed, a flower bulb, or slips from a pretty foliage plant. Wrapped candies or small cookies may be used, too, but they are not in the true spirit of May Day—a celebration of growth and fertility.

When the baskets are finished and filled with May Day surprises, hang them on the doors of friends and neighbors. Carry them to a friend who is ill or shut in. But save the most beautiful basket for a loved one. You might receive a kiss for your efforts.

May Day Song

We've been rambling all the night
    And some time of this day
And now returning back again,
    We bring a garland gay.

A garland gay we bring you here,
    And at your door we stand;
It is a sprout, well-budded out,
    The work of our Lord's hand.

N. P. WILLIS

Iris blooming along a fence beside a country road in Charlottesville, Virginia. Photo copyright William H. Johnson, Johnson's Photography (44774-00107).

The Celebration 1906

Josie Churchill

We hold these truths to be self-evident,

that all men are created equal . . .

–U.S. Declaration of Independence

On July 4th, 1906, we were eating an early breakfast for today would be about the most important holiday of the year. . . . Because these were horse-and-buggy days, Fourth of July celebrations dotted the country. Patriotism was at a high pitch.

Papa informed us we would be leaving about 10 o'clock that morning. My little brother and I could hardly wait for him to hitch Flory, our bay mare, to the buggy and leave for the celebration grounds in the maple grove which surrounded the Sugar Grove School.

Mama had prepared our picnic dinner, which we always ate with relatives. Papa had combed the woods and fence rows for enough berries for a pie. He used to say, "A blackcap pie for the Fourth of July," and he usually managed to find them. . . .

For the Fourth of July celebration, everyone dressed in his best. Sewing machines had been humming for days and often into the night to complete some needed garment. Mama had bought the yard goods for our dresses from an itinerant peddler.

He was Namer Shaheen, and he had an established route from La Crosse through Middle Ridge, Cashton, Westby, and the rural areas. His horse and buckboard turned into our driveway several times a year. A welcomed guest! Wherever he stopped, he was escorted to the door by gleeful children eager to see what was in those big black valises. Namer's horse, Mellie, loved the sugar the children fed her as she nibbled away at grass in the yard.

No one wanted to miss "Old Namer" when he unfolded those cases on the floor. Funny, but Papa always seemed to need a rest right at this moment.

Those cases contained notions, ribbons, laces and thread, thimbles, needles and pins, combs, shoestrings, penknives, handkerchiefs, and mouth organs, as well as delightful necklaces with heart-shaped lockets which held little pink cakes of perfume. And there were yard goods. Silks, calico, gingham, and chambrays. His valises also held shirts, suspenders, celluloid collars, socks, and underwear.

Namer Shaheen fulfilled a great need for country people. While he brought many items to us for purchase, he did not supply the fancy decorated hats that were worn by little girls and their mamas. Mine was cream-colored straw covered with crimped chiffon and around the crown was a wreath of blue forget-me-nots.

Our road led us up a steep hill through the woods, where basswood trees were alive with bees sipping at the creamy white blossoms that were practically dripping with honey. When we stopped to let Flory rest, Papa would scan the hillside and muse, "I'm going to look here for a bee tree one of these days." He kept us supplied with wild honey all summer and fall. . . .

By the time we reached the grove, we were part of a caravan of topbuggies, surreys, buckboards, and wagons. Horses were unhitched and tied to the rigs in the fringe of the woods where they could eat their noon oats.

Fluttering flags decorated the speaker's stand upon which had been erected benches for honored guests. Among these were our local Civil War veterans.

My great uncle, Sam McDaniel, was one of them. His crutches were neatly placed beside him. They had been near him for forty-four years now, since he had lost his leg at the Battle of Monterey, Virginia, on April 12, 1862. Some worthy student recited the Declaration of Independence. Candidates for county offices made political speeches, and sometimes contenders for the state Assembly or Senate managed to call at several of these celebrations, informing us of how our tax money was being squandered down in Madison.

Our local minister spoke of God's grace and the blessings of living in a free land and then gave the benediction. All this was accompanied by renditions of "America," "The Star Spangled-Banner," and "Tenting Tonight" by a fife and drum corps.

A couple of small stands, decorated with red, white, and blue bunting, sold treats and firecrackers. White tablecloths were spread on the ground in many shady spots. We ate our dinner with about twenty uncles, aunts, and cousins.

In the early afternoon a little band led a parade of clowning ragamuffins. Men pitched horseshoes and boys climbed greased poles to get a dollar bill at the top.

But the part that interested Papa most was the dance bowery under the big maple trees. This was a family enterprise managed by four brothers-in-law. They operated this for several years, constructing it from fitted lumber which they stored from year to year.

Their bowery was decorated with many flags, and seats had been built all around it, except where the roofed-over music stand was attached. Into this Uncle Walter, who was a music teacher, had moved the pump organ he would play.

Over the floor, fine paraffin shavings had been spread. With the summer's warmth the dance floor was soon as slick as glass. Leafy shadows silently danced across the smooth floor, coaxing one to participate.

Dapper Uncle Sonny, a professional caller, began calling the dances, and soon waltzes, two-steps, schottisches, quadrilles, and square dances commenced and would continue until long after midnight to the tunes of "Those Golden Slippers," "Red Wing," and "Down in the Diving Bell."

Mama drove Flory out of the grove with two protesting children. Papa would come when it was all over. And so it was!

Starch Magic

Eva Augustin Rumpf

Man works from sun to sun, but woman's work is never done. —AUTHOR UNKNOWN

Remember starch? Anyone who grew up before polyester surely does. It was starch that added refinement to dress, made one presentable in polite society, and separated the spiffy from the slovenly. The weak modern stuff in the spray can on today's supermarket shelves doesn't qualify. Real starch was hard, blue, and came in a big block with indentations like a candy bar, so you could break off sections.

Starching and ironing the family wash took the better part of the block of starch and the day as well. As a young child, I trailed my mother from kitchen to wash shed to yard and back again as she performed this weekly chore. She would start a big pot of water heating on the gas stove, then head out to the shed behind our house. There the wringer washing machine *ka-chunked* the dirt out of the clothes while my mother filled a rinse tub with fresh water.

Then, piece by piece, she guided the clothes through the wringer to squeeze out the soapy water, letting them splash down into the rinse tub below. Up and down, in the rinse water they were dunked, until the last of the soap was out of each item. Through the wringer they went again and plopped into the waiting basket like flat, dead fish. Next came a further sorting process as the starchables were separated from the rest of the batch. Socks, underwear, towels, sheets, and old clothes not fit to be worn in public went to the clothesline, where they took on the slightly stiff feel and the fresh, wholesome smell of outdoor drying.

Meanwhile, the starch pot was steaming on the stove. Mom knew just how many starch blocks to break off and drop into the pot. She turned off the gas and stirred the steaming cauldron with a long-handled spoon. As the starch dissolved, the water turned cloudy and thickened. The potion was ready to work its magic.

Carefully, my mother carried the pot to the shed and poured it into a wash tub. Using a sawed-off broom handle, she dipped each article of clothing into the hot solution until it was evenly saturated with starchy water. She lifted the stick, and the steam rose from the soaked clothing, filling the air with a clean, sweet fragrance. She gingerly squeezed the fabric,

Sugar maples in glorious color set off weathered barns in Kewaunee County, Wisconsin. Photo copyright Darryl Beers (MT-01J59-66).

and the still warm, sticky water oozed out and trickled over her hands and back into the tub. Dad's cotton work shirts and pants needed the strongest dose, so they were dipped first. Then came our Sunday outfits and school clothes. Less significant items were saved till last, in case we ran short and the starch had to be stretched out by adding more water.

Finally, the starched clothes were ready to be hung on the lines in the backyard to dry. I was fascinated to see the shirts and dresses petrify as they dried, turning into stiff, grotesque statues, faceless and limbless. It was fun to take the long, full skirts from the line and stand them on the grass like giant bells, misshapen and silent.

But the life span of these frozen oddities was short indeed, for within a few hours they were scooped up, taken inside, and mercilessly crushed into a pile on the kitchen table. There, they were subjected to the sprinkler, a water-filled Coke bottle, topped with an aluminum cap full of tiny holes. After the sprinkling, each item was rolled into a tight, log-shaped bundle and stuffed into a plastic bag. If the ironing wasn't finished the same day, the damp clothes in the bag would keep nicely in the refrigerator for a day or two.

But even then this weekly ritual was drawing to a close. Suddenly "wash and wear" fabrics became the rage, and everyone pretended they looked just as good as the old starched and ironed ones. Before long, polyester and other miracle fibers ushered in permanent press and made starching and ironing as we knew them obsolete. Irons became wimpy, lightweight "touch-up" tools. Blocks of starch disappeared from grocery shelves, taking with them their secrets and depriving new generations of children from witnessing the magic they worked.

The Picnic to the Hills

EDNA JAQUES

The picnic to the hills was the highlight of the summer. We always held it on the first of July. It was the only outing of the year.

I couldn't sleep a wink the night before; I would just lie there in bed with my little sister, getting up a dozen times to look out the little narrow window and see if it was getting daylight, maybe drop off to sleep for a few minutes and then spring up again and see dawn coming up across the flats. And there is no more glorious sight on this earth than the sun slowly rising on the prairie, filling the summer world with colors that defy description. First a faint pink, then the full blooming of dawn—green, orange, yellow and always that sense of wonder at the vastness of the earth from rim to rim—empty and silent, yet filled with a strange breathing like wings above the house.

Meadow larks would be piping their songs, hundreds of them. The rooster would let out a few squawks; the dog would shake himself and wander towards the barn, as if to reassure himself that all was well; the hens would come out of the hen house door, ruffling their wings and start to hunt for food. The old cow on her tether would rise and stretch and start to eat as if to say, "Well, get up everyone. It's another day."

By this time we three girls would be dressed. There were no "outfits" for us, just nice little print dresses, the good ones we had been saving for the occasion. . . .

Breakfast would be a hurried meal: good oatmeal porridge, big slices of homemade bread with syrup, and homemade butter. Water would be left in pans in the yard for the chickens; the milk would be strained and set in blue pans in the cellar; the mother hens were left in their little overnight houses with slats for the little chickens to run in and out; the pigs were fed with extra rations; cows were freshly tethered on their long ropes and horses were fed.

My mother would have made most of the lunch the night before and packed in the blue bread pan: homemade head cheese, potato salad, radishes and little green onions, and maybe a bit of leftover Christmas cake, a raisin pie, and her good homemade cookies.

Old Kit and Farmer would be hitched to the lumber wagon with dad and maw on the spring seat, we three in the back of the wagon as usual, laughing and wild with excitement. . . . The trail headed due south, winding here and there with a little curve around a gopher or badger hole. Ahead, the hills would beckon, rising blue and lovely against the sky.

Cow parsnips beside a stump in a meadow during a July morning drizzle on Shrine Mountain in the Gore Range of the White River National Forest, Colorado. Photo copyright Jeff Gnass (21-2383-482).

4-H BEST FRESH STRAWBERRY BUNDT CAKE

Makes 10 to 12 servings

1½ cups sliced fresh strawberries	¾ cup butter, room temperature
3 cups plus 1 tablespoon all-purpose flour	2 cups sugar
1 tablespoon baking powder	3 large eggs
½ teaspoon salt	¾ cup milk
	Powdered sugar

Preheat oven to 350° F. Grease and lightly flour a 12-cup bundt pan; set aside. In a small bowl, toss strawberries with 1 tablespoon flour; set aside. In a large bowl, sift together 3 cups of the flour, baking powder, and salt; set aside. In a large bowl, cream butter and granulated sugar on high speed of electric mixer until light. Add eggs, one at a time, beating well after each addition. Alternately add flour mixture and milk to butter mixture. Carefully fold strawberries into batter. Pour batter into prepared pan. Bake for 1 hour and fifteen minutes or until a wooden pick inserted near the center comes out clean. Cool in pan on wire rack for 15 minutes. Turn out onto wire rack to cool completely. Sprinkle cake with sifted powdered sugar. Serve with additional sweetened sliced strawberries, if desired.

BLUE RIBBON BAKING

CHAMPIONSHIP CHERRY COBBLER

Makes 6 servings

4 cups canned tart cherries, undrained	2 tablespoons butter
1 cup sugar	⅛ teaspoon salt
2 tablespoon quick-cooking tapioca	4 drops almond extract

Preheat oven to 400° F. In a medium saucepan, combine cherries and liquid, sugar, and tapioca. Cook over low heat for about 15 minutes, stirring constantly, until thickened and clear. Stir in butter, salt, and almond extract. Pour hot cherry mixture into a 10- x 6- x 1½-inch baking dish. Drop COBBLER TOPPING by spoonfuls over cherry mixture. Bake 20 minutes, or until crust is golden brown. Cool on wire rack. Serve with cream or vanilla ice cream.

Cobbler Topping

1 cup all-purpose flour	¼ cup butter
1 tablespoon sugar	¼ cup milk
1½ teaspoons baking powder	1 large egg, lightly beaten
¼ teaspoons salt	

In a small mixing bowl, sift together flour, sugar, baking powder, and salt. Cut in butter with pastry blender or two knives until mixture resembles coarse crumbs. In a small bowl, whisk together milk and egg. Add liquid mixture to dry ingredients; stir just until moistened.

First Prize Country-Style Apple Pie

Makes 6 to 8 servings

1 recipe double pie crust	Pinch ground nutmeg
5 cups (5 to 6 apples) sliced baking apples, such as Granny Smith	1 large egg white, beaten with
1 tablespoon lemon juice	1 tablespoon water
¾ cup granulated sugar	1 to 2 tablespoons chilled unsalted butter, cut into small pieces
1½ tablespoons cornstarch	Cheddar cheese slices
1 teaspoon ground cinnamon	

Prepare your favorite piecrust. Roll out half the dough and fit into a 9-inch pie plate. Roll out remaining portion; fold into quarters. Use a sharp knife to cut three slits on both of the straight sides of the dough. Place crust on a plate; cover both crusts with plastic wrap and refrigerate until ready to use.

Preheat oven to 450° F. In a small bowl, combine sugar, cornstarch, cinnamon, and nutmeg; set aside. Peel, core, and cut apples into thick slices. Toss apple slices lightly in lemon juice, then coat with sugar mixture. Remove prepared bottom pie crust from refrigerator. Brush bottom and sides with egg-white mixture. Pour apples into crust. Dot with butter. Gently unfold top crust on top of apples. Trim overhang to 1 inch. Moisten edges of both crusts. Press edges together and turn under. Crimp edges. (Top crust can be decorated with leftover pieces of pastry dough cut into shapes, if desired. Moisten undersides with water to attach to crust.) Brush top crust with remaining egg white. Place pie on rack in middle of oven. Reduce heat to 350° F. Bake 1 hour, or until bubbly and crust is golden brown. Cool on wire rack. Serve warm with a thin slice of Cheddar cheese on each slice.

Huskings, Quiltings, and Barn Raisings

VICTORIA SHERROW

The only way to have a friend is to be one. –RALPH WALDO EMERSON

New neighbors! To people living in sparsely settled areas in early America, these two words carried excitement. The arrival of new settlers enabled people to hear news about their former homelands or about other parts of the country. It also meant that everyone living within several miles around the area would soon gather to help the new arrivals clear their land and build a home, and perhaps a barn. . . .

In 1795, a Vermont settler wrote about an unfortunate but not uncommon event in his neighborhood:

> Mr. Stephen Hollister's barn was burned by sparks blowing from a neighbor's clearing. The neighbors who rallied at the burning determined that he should have a new barn. They scattered to invite others and to return with tools, team, provisions, etc., next morning. . . . The timber was cut, hewed, framed, and raised in a day; and before the ruins were done smoking, a new barn frame, 30 feet by 40 feet, was ready for covering.

This diary entry, quoted by Bertha S. Dodge in *Tales of Vermont Ways and People*, shows how settlers united in times of trouble. Fires occurred frequently in early America and led to the damage and loss of both homes and barns. Usually, however, a barn raising signaled a happier occasion—for example, a marriage or the arrival of a new family in the area. Barn raisings were among the most festive work-play parties. People of all ages participated in the work, feasting, and fun. . . .

Cornhusking parties involved both men and women. At harvest time, neighbors usually met at dusk in the barn and sat around a long pile of corn. They formed two teams, sometimes choosing members by flipping a chip that had been made by leaving bark on one side and filing the other side smooth. The team leaders then agreed on how to divide the corn pile into equal parts, placing a marker in the middle.

THE IDEALS COUNTRY TREASURY

As the contest began, fingers moved quickly and dozens of ears hit the door. Some workers used husking pins—small spikes fastened across their palms—to help them remove the outer leaves of the corn. The huskers talked, joked, and sang folk songs as they hurried to finish their pile first.

Occasionally, a young man found a red ear in his corn. This permitted him to kiss a girl . . . When a girl found a red ear, she could hand it to her favorite young man and receive a kiss from him. Married people kissed each other. Some unattached young men took care to hide a red ear in their pockets before going "a-husking." . . .

Often, only women attended [apple bees], forming a circle around a washtub, with aprons tied over their homespun or calico dresses. They shared stories, recipes, songs, and common problems as they pared and sliced, tossing the peels and fruit into separate pans and baskets placed around the kitchen. . . .

One of the best-known work-play parties, the quilting bee, has been the object of songs, stories, and poems. The famous nineteenth-century American composer, Stephen Foster, featured this work-play party in one of his folk songs:

> In the sky the bright stars glittered,
> On the banks the pale moon shone,
> And 'twas from Aunt Dinah's quilting party,
> I was seeing Nellie home. . . .

Quilting bees let women socialize and use their artistic and sewing skills, while providing household essentials. Often, quilts were the brightest and most individual items in pioneer homes. They used fabric that might otherwise have been discarded. Old clothes sewn in gave the quilts sentimental value too—as when scraps of Grandmother's wedding dress, a military coat, or a baby's christening gown were passed on in family quilts. Even scraps less than one-inch square were used, with one quilt from the early 1800s containing 30,000 such tiny pieces. . . .

Quilting bees were mostly winter events and were one of the few approved social outings for women. The quiltings often took place at the largest home nearby. Women brought their completed quilt tops and linings the same size, ready to be tied to a frame and sewn to the bottom layer.

Besides making quilts together, the settlers met to perform other tasks that would provide clothing and bedding. Some frontier people wore clothing made from animal skins—deer, raccoon, squirrel, rabbit, bear, or buffalo—but wool was the main fabric used for clothing. Clothes were made of wool or linen (from the flax plant) or a combination of these called linsey-woolsey.

Cloth making began in the spring, when the sheep, wearing thick winter coats, were led to the riverbank to be washed. A mixture of tobacco and water was sometimes used, because it killed the bugs living in the sheep's fleece. Children who helped with this chore could enjoy going for a swim after they finished. . . .

The end of this frolic was often marked with popcorn and a taffy pull for the young people. Supper included roast goose, venison, biscuits, gingerbread, cider, and hot coffee. After a dance, the families returned home by sleigh or on foot.

In early America, people building new lives in new settlements relied on work-play parties to meet their basic needs. Today, people can meet those same needs by visiting numerous well-stocked stores. Yet quilting bees, sewing circles, harvest festivals, and the like are still popular. Although people today do not always need these events to survive, they like to socialize with neighbors and take part in community life. . . . So, despite the hectic pace of modern life or perhaps because of it—people continue to plan ways to work and play together.

Sugaring Time

ERIC SLOANE

$\mathcal{N}$o early American season was more definite than sugaring time. The right time is usually between mid-March and mid-April, when the sap is flowing properly. Then the nights are cold enough to freeze sharply and the days warm enough to thaw freely. . . . The thermometer must not rise above forty degrees by day, nor sink below twenty-four degrees at night. It is this magic see-sawing between winter and spring that decides the sugaring season. . . .

Let John Burroughs describe the art of maple sugaring:

> Maple sugar in its perfection is rarely seen, perhaps never seen, in the market. When made in large quantities and indifferently, it is dark and coarse; but when made in small quantities—that is, quickly from the first run of sap and properly treated—it has a wild delicacy of flavor that no other sweet can match. What you smell in freshly cut maple wood, or taste in the blossom of the tree, is in it. It is then, indeed, the distilled essence of the tree. Made into syrup, it is white and clear as clover honey; and crystallized into sugar, it is pure as the wax. The way to attain this result is to evaporate the sap under cover in an enameled kettle; when reduced about twelve times, allow it to settle half a day or more; then clarify with milk or the white of an egg. The product is virgin syrup . . .

107

Possibly, breeding could have done for the maple tree what has been done for the sugar beet and sugar cane, to make its yield greater. But the slow-growing maple is not adapted to the speed of modern farming; it takes forty to fifty years before a tree is in full production. The experimentation, selection, breeding, and grafting done with any common fruit tree has never been afforded the American maple. Its sugar has been taken for two centuries without benefit of any research into cultivation, yet with no loss to the trees. Despite our tremendous increase in population two hundred years ago there was four times the amount of maple sugar and syrup produced each year as there is now. Sugaring was hard work, but the American farmer made such a cheerful season of it that the whole family looked forward to sugaring, making it more play than work.

Sugar maple trees with sap buckets in Hebron, New Hampshire. Photo copyright William H. Johnson, Johnson's Photography (23046-00113).

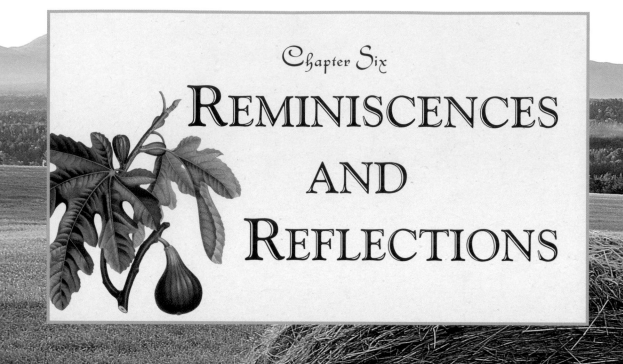

Chapter Six

REMINISCENCES AND REFLECTIONS

The Charm of Water Mills

BETH HUWILER

The water mill is one of the most charming and widespread relics of early American culture. If you travel through the countryside, particularly in the East, you are likely to see an occasional mill nestled beside a rippling stream. Although the years may have halted the spinning of the wheel and spread moss over the adjacent building, mills still offer a sense of the activity that once made it the hub of the community. In fact, it was not uncommon for towns to be charted around mills, as indicated by the number of towns with "Mill" as part of their names.

Mills originated in prehistoric times—when people first began grinding grain for bread. Archaeologists have discovered primitive mills—simple stone slabs—that ground grain more than nine thousand years ago. These forerunners of modern mills usually consisted of two stones rubbed together, the grain between them. After a time, the bottom stone would begin to wear away, leaving a hollow in the center that made the process more efficient. Soon millstones were made with a hollow in the bottom stone.

There were refinements in the milling process throughout the nineteenth century. Water became a major source of power until the invention of the steam engine; and stones were used to grind the grain until the mid-1800s.

The bread you bake with flour ground the old-fashioned way might not taste any better than bread made with store-bought flour, but chances are that it will. Maybe it's the magic of doing things the traditional way, the country way. It could be the best bread you've ever eaten.

Autumn time at Glade Creek Grist Mill in Babcock State Park, West Virginia. Photo copyright Dick Dietrich (6177-626).

Weather Vanes

JOHN A. NELSON

When it is evening, ye say,
It will be fair weather: for
the sky is red. —MATTHEW 16:2

Human beings have always wanted to know which way the wind blows. Perhaps early man simply wanted to avoid the smoke from his fires that blew into his face. Knowing wind direction also helped early man to predict the weather, which directly affected most of his daily activities.

The Greeks provided the first record of a weather vane. This weather vane was in the shape of Triton, the half-man, half-fish god of the sea. It stood atop the octagonal Tower of the Winds, which was built in Athens in the first century A.D.

Archaeological evidence demonstrates that early Viking ships also used wind indicators. Weather vanes came to Europe in the Middle Ages. The early European weather vanes reflected the heraldic traditions of medieval castles, often bearing the insignia of the feudal lords.

In colonial America weather vane motifs were limited to a few basic designs: a simple arrow, a rooster or cock, a fish, an Indian, a grasshopper. After the colonies obtained independence from England, designs began to reflect special or local interest. Churches used Christian symbols, such as a cock, a fish, or an angel. Farmers used livestock themes to adorn their houses and barns: horses, cows, sheep, pigs, hens, and roosters. Along the seacoast, fish, whales, ships, and even serpents were popular.

Early originals were made of pine that was carved to the desired form. Later, craftsmen cut thin sheets of iron, zinc, or tin to shape with a hammer and chisel. Even later, weather vanes were made of soft copper or bronze. These usually had hollow bodies. A simple half-mold was carved into a piece of wood, and the copper or bronze was beaten into the half-mold. The two halves were then soldered together to create a three-dimensional, hollow body.

Many early hollow-bodied weather vanes contained written messages from their original makers. The name of the maker, the date, the recipient, and other pertinent infor-

Sunset over cupolas with weather vanes in Bristol, New Hampshire. Photo copyright William H. Johnson, Johnson's Photography (23089-00501).

mation about the vane might be included. If the weather vane was repaired, that craftsman might add to the note. Even now, some fortunate owners are finding these messages in their weather vanes.

The local carvers and metalworkers who made these weather vanes were concerned with the functionality of their designs. The pointer's shape had to be broad enough to catch the wind, with more surface area on the side opposite the indicator. A rooster made an excellent pointer: the tail feathers offered a large surface area to the wind, which swung the vane around until the beak pointed into the wind, indicating its direction.

The pointer's shape needed to balance on the pivot point. Hollow-bodied weather vanes were easy to balance. Molten lead could be poured into the hollow body wherever necessary to balance the vane. Flat silhouette designs were slightly harder to balance because of the difficulty in hiding the counterbalance material. Thin strips of lead were attached to the lighter side in such a way as to be nearly invisible from the ground.

An early New England maker of weather vanes was once asked if he could build a weather vane that would indicate the velocity as well as the direction of the wind. The craftsman is reported to have told his customer, "What we use around these parts is a length of chain. When the chain stands out straight, there's a

gale a-blowin'." This joke became famous, and in fact, many colonial weather vanes contain a chain somewhere in their structure.

Most early wooden weather vanes were painted white, Indian red, or yellow ocher. The ocher was used to simulate gilt. Some were painted with bold, bright colors. Metal weather vanes were painted or gilded. As for wooden weather vanes, yellow ocher was often used in place of gilt or gold leaf. Some metal vanes were left unpainted, but most had a coat of dark brown or black so that they would create a bold silhouette against the sky. Copper weather vanes were left unpainted and allowed to weather to a beautiful soft gray.

Today, weather vanes not only tell us which way the wind blows, but, perhaps more importantly, provide a link to the past—to the days before television weathermen. Weather vanes—whether copper or painted, sea creature or barnyard fowl—warm our hearts as we look past their directional pointers and back to the days when the weather was sometimes the most important subject of the day.

Carry Me
Back to the Farm

MARJORIE HOLMES

What we remember from childhood, we remember forever—permanent ghosts, stamped, imprinted, eternally seen. –CYNTHIA OZICK

For children raised in city or suburbs there is nothing more fascinating than a farm. The elementary school my youngsters attended staged an annual pilgrimage for the sole purpose of letting pupils hear cows moo and pigs grunt, pet sheep, hold baby ducklings, and see chickens live and clucking about instead of prone in a supermarket. And many farmers do a nice seasonal business by taking on a few kids or even whole families for an old-fashioned summer vacation on a farm.

Farms were a part of my childhood's landscape, a way of life in our town. Farms flowed all about us and right down to the lake on the opposite shores. Five minutes from Main Street you were flanked by fields and pastures, vast loamy acres that were black with plowing in spring and fall, shimmering green and gold all summer, with windmills rising like slender chrysanthemums against the open sky. . . .

Practically all our relatives lived on farms, and both my parents had been born in the country. Mother's parents moved to town when she was a little girl, so she felt she had escaped what was to her, for some reason, an appalling fate. She loathed and detested farms. The most miserable year of her life, she claimed, was the one when Dad, full of ebullient hopes, had persuaded her to "go on the farm." "It rained every day and ruined the corn, and we lost everything we had," she claimed. Mother wept almost as copiously as the skies. At last, hopes drenched, they moved back to town.

Most of my father's life, he served farmers in some capacity, selling them cream separators or incubators or tractors, bargaining with their wives for chickens, or managing Vic Sjostrom's big poultry house. Nonetheless we felt vastly superior to country kids, including our numerous cousins. This did not diminish our delight in going to visit them, where we pretended a pretty ignorance of rural ways, and it pleased us to no end that they resented us and called us

114

names like "Stuck up" and "City slickers."

Our favorite cousins to visit were the Pattens, distant relatives on Mother's side. Old Tom, as we called him, owned half the county but he enjoyed playing the curmudgeon, resisting cars and gravel roads, scolding, "People oughta stay home where they belong." Three sons were still on the farm when we spent our summer vacations among them, and they seemed to us truly giants upon their earth, in fearless command of windmills and threshing machines and monstrous plodding horses. . . . They rigged up a giant swing for us in the maple tree and pushed us to terrifying heights. They taught us to milk, or tried to, laughing at our tipsy perch on the one-legged stool, our feeble efforts to squeeze a drop or two from the dust leather teats. (How merrily the pail rang when they took over, how the warm foam rose!) They amused us by sending jets of milk toward the mouths of the hovering cats.

They boosted us up into the haymow and patiently came after us when we were scared to come down. They let us climb the silver scaffolding of the windmill. Our brother climbed fearlessly to the very wheel sometimes and touched its magical blades. I never got beyond the first platform. It trembled and swayed slightly, as if in gentle warning. Above, its mystical head seemed to be looking left and right, a genteel pompadoured lady with a comb in her hair, visiting with the wind and watching for something in the sky. That this elegant personage provided the power to suck up water from the well and bring it into great moss-grown tanks and troughs where thirsty stock drank only added to the marvel.

We gathered eggs for Cousin Louie, setting forth with baskets, to hunt them in nests and mangers, a veritable Easter morning every day. Sometimes the fragile globes were new-laid and still warm. We were warned to stay clear of the setting hens—their yellow beaks would stab if you tried to disturb their precious clutch. We walked gingerly, carrying this rare cargo, perhaps unconsciously recognizing its worth. For every farm wife was expected to raise chickens, and the egg money was usually considered hers (in that way she often had more financial independence than her sisters in town). . . . A cream separator stood in every pantry; hers the job of operating this contraption, and cleaning it, and churning the butter, most of which was carried to town and sold along with the eggs on Saturday.

Each morning we also ran or sauntered a half mile down the road to get the mail. Grasshoppers, jewel-green, dropped like bullets in the ruts at our bare feet, butterflies twinkled, red or gold-winged blackbirds flocked in the pastures. From barbed-wire fences meadowlarks sang. Along the road telephone wires hummed. You could hear them clearly if you pressed your ears against the hot wooden poles. It was like listening to distant voices in mysterious conversation, as if the very poles were humming and throbbing to the secret words people were saying to each other.

There was something melancholy and yet reassuring about it; the country could be so lonely. In a farmhouse the incessant ringing of the telephone both relieved and yet somehow enhanced the loneliness. You kept listening for your own ring, or the ring of neighbors on your party line, and if the loneliness got too bad you could "rubber." This meant carefully picking up the receiver and listening in. Sometimes people got so interested they forgot and *butted* into the conversation. . . .

The farm stretched farther than the eye could follow. And at its corner was assembled a veritable village of buildings—practically every one of them bigger than the cramped cottage that housed the family. The long pig-house with its squealing, grunting, dozing, rooting occupants who spilled over into the rutted lot, there to wallow in muddy spills or trip about, curly

tails jaunty, and strangely dainty on their cleft high heels. The musky-smelling cowshed where the heavy-uddered creatures were relieved of their burden morning and night. The brooder house and chicken house, smelling of feathers and chicken dirt and lime. In addition there were the corncribs, the machine sheds, the silos and granary, and an immense barn.

All this to be explored, hidden in, played in, while in adjacent dusky groves and fragrant humming weedy lots could be found an assortment of abandoned buggies, corn-planters, harrows, discs, and other machines worthy of an amusement park.

The barn was our favorite place, however, and we usually saved it for afternoon. The barn was like the castle on the grounds, its haymow surely the place where Rumpelstiltskin spun flax into gold. Anyway, here the straw and hay were piled, great fluffy drifts of it, a veritable sea in which to wallow. Bales of hay were stacked to the rafters, and these we arranged into steps and platforms to leap from. There was also a long rope tied to an overhead beam, with a metal hook at its end. By grasping this and kicking off, we could soar almost out the open haydoor that framed the sky, before dropping. The hay was sweet and dusty and tickling. Swallows darted in and out, pigeons strutted, crooning. Below, we could hear a few horses in their stalls, while outside, from the shimmering meadows came the plaintive, lonely call of mourning doves.

Finally, when we were done with jumping and swinging and screeching hayfights, we would climb on the broad wooden gates to the pasture and watch for the men coming in from the fields. With a glad shout, we'd run to meet them, begging for a ride. Grinning good-naturedly, they would boost us onto the broad slippery backs. The horses had a rank-sweet vinegary odor; we clung to their dry brittle manes or a knob of the jingling harness while our cousins led the beasts to the watering tank, where they bent their heads to drink great noisy slobbering draughts of

the bitter-cold water. Then plonk-plonk-plonk up to the barn and through its half-open divided doors. Their hooves struck out a kind of puddingy music on the bare earth floors. The smell of manure and hay and horse and harness made the nostrils tingle.

Now the dreamy afternoon quality of the barn changed, came suddenly strongly alive. There was a brisk sound of buckets clanking, the whisking of pitchforks and hay, the rumble and rattle of ears of corn being dumped into the feeding bins. While over all would settle the rich and rhythmic harmonies of great teeth munching.

Swallows in the Barn

I can smell the fragrant mow
    On a sultry summer day
When I scrambled up somehow
    To hide slyly in the hay.

There were columns of spun gold
    Sifting through the weathered roof,
For the barn was very old
    And the sunbeams were the proof.

When a barn is weathered gray
    And I chance to pass it by,
Then I wonder if today
    It would seem so nobly high,

And if summer finds a boy,
    Barefoot, drowsy, who believes
In the tales of purest joy
    Told by swallows in the eaves!

ANNE CAMPBELL

117

Gambrel barn with wooden shingles amid a field of wildflowers in Colebrook, New Hampshire. Photo copyright William H. Johnson, Johnson's Photography (53006-00108).

Antique Bridges

RAYMOND SCHUESSLER

Memory is the diary that we all carry with us. —OSCAR WILDE

There's hardly a kid in America who grows up not knowing what a covered bridge is—knowing but not really seeing. There are hundreds of renditions in books, but unless you've hiked or driven pretty extensively, the odds are against your actually seeing one. Thousands of them have either burned, rotted or simply been torn down. . . .

Wooden bridges first became part of the American scene late in the 1700s and early 1800s, . . . constructed by laying poles over fallen logs. As these unprotected structures soon weakened, they added supporting trusses and a roof to help protect them against the weather. Some were built by the community; others were privately built as toll bridges. Churchgoers crossed free on Sundays; a passenger on foot was charged one cent; a horse and rider, four cents; a cow, one cent; and sheep or swine, a half cent.

As time wore on, bridges creaked under the weight of ox-drawn carts when the country was largely wilderness. They clattered beneath the pounding hooves of saddle mounts and wagons. Without them, the West would have been won much more slowly and because of them, railroads penetrated the wilderness more rapidly.

But why were the bridges covered? It was not, as one European visitor exclaimed, that "Americans have a quaint custom of building barns atop their bridges." But more as a farmer explained, "For the same reason women wear long skirts—to protect the underpinning." Quite simply, the roof protected the large supporting timbers from the rotting effects of sun and rain. After all, a covered bridge had a life expectancy of eighty years, whereas one left uncovered lasted only ten.

Covered bridges were practical as well as long-lived. Farmers driving their stock to market normally had trouble persuading cattle to cross open bridges. When the same bridges were covered, the cattle entered happily, expecting to be fed inside. Allowing no reflection from the water below, the covered structures also cut down on the number of accidents caused from shying horses.

The basic principle for construction is credited to Theodore Burr, an American of Torringford, Connecticut, who developed it in 1798 (patented in 1817). Fundamentally, it is that of the king post truss. The

118

longest timbers are used as diagonals, meeting in the center at the top of the vertical post. The base of the triangle thus formed is longer than available timber and made of two timbers each shorter than the diagonals.

Most of the New York State bridges now standing used the Town Lattice Truss which was patented in 1820 and 1835 by Ithiel Town, an architect of New Haven, Connecticut. It consists of planks joined together with wooden pins in a lattice pattern. Since it used lighter timbers than other styles—and was easier and cheaper to build—it soon became the most popular design.

Aside from being just about the best advertising media of their day, they were frequently the town meeting place as well. Here is an account of one of the last bridges near Cedarburg, Wisconsin.

"It was always a great gathering place.

There was a good swimming hole right beneath it in the creek and many is the time we girls changed our clothes in the privacy of that bridge. The grove along the creek banks was a popular picnic place. In case of rain, they simply moved the picnic onto the bridge, under the timbers. In wintertime, people used it for skating from and warming themselves. . . ."

There are numerous sinister tales as well: stories of hangings and highwaymen who lurked in the shadows of windowless darkness to prey on travelers. But there were laws to protect people, just as there were laws requiring towns to "snow" bridges—that is to shovel snow onto the floors of covered bridges for sleighs and sleds.

Covered bridge over the Sunday River near the village of Newry, Maine. Photo copyright Jeff Gnass (25-2339-403).

119

REMINISCENCES AND REFLECTIONS

Roadside Memories

DONALD S. HENNING

Those who see the countryside only as they rush by on the highway miss the chance to enjoy nature at its serene best and to make more discoveries in an hour than they might in a year. In my lifetime, some of the moments I treasure most were spent strolling leisurely along an unpaved country road, with its bordering fences and unspoiled abundance of flora and fauna.

Still vivid in my memory are the visits to my uncle's farm. When I was old enough to leave the yard, I would wander down the deadened, narrow dirt road across from the house. I have only to shut my eyes, and I'm back there. It is a clear day in July, and it would be hot except for the breeze from Lake Michigan, a few miles away.

The road is magical to a city boy though it is no more than a pair of dusty ruts with a ridge of grass, dandelions, and plantain between. How many trips have wagon wheels and Model T tires made down this lane, I wonder, to cause such deep tracks?

As I walk, a chipmunk, tall erect, scurries across my path and into a thick tangle of grapevines covering the ground. Experimentally, I tug at some leaves where the animal disappeared, and the whole mass of grapevines moves. Some vines are also clinging by tendrils to the weathered silver-gray wooden posts and rusty barbed wire of the fence, and I can see the clusters of grapes that are forming. Butter-and-eggs, like miniature yellow and orange snapdragons, line the road on either side, much more hardy and profuse than their larger cousins in our garden at home. Rising from the undergrowth are huge bunches of coneflowers and daisies. Spotted white cabbage butterflies flit from one blossom to the next. The breeze pauses momentarily, and I am suddenly aware of the buzzing of honeybees and the deeper droning of bumblebees all along the roadside. Shimmering dragonflies skim erratically over velvety cattails where the road goes past a little marshy area. Across the way, a few monarch butterflies hover around a patch of milkweed, The noisy twittering of a flock of sparrows in a hawthorn tree just over the fence draws my attention, and nearby I see graceful Queen Anne's lace and stalks of blue chicory. . . .

Though I have enjoyed the pleasures of similar roadside worlds many times throughout the years,that special afternoon a half-century ago is always there in memory—vivid and peaceful and warm.

Queen Anne's lace, daisies, yarrow, and common mullein at St. John's wort, near Poultney, Vermont. Photo copyright William H. Johnson, Johnson's Photography (24698-00102).

What Is the Country?

PATRICIA MAXWELL

Bliss in possession will not last;

Remembered joys are never past.

–JAMES MONTGOMERY

The country is something to run away from, or something to cling to; it is magic or monotony, depending on the person. It is a composite of the beginning and ending of mankind, a changing panorama of sights and sounds and smell and emotions.

The country in spring is tiny purple and white flowers peeping through the fresh, tender grass; the sour taste of juicy "sour grass" crunching between the teeth; the dewy sweet smell of violets along a mossy creek; the haunting fragrance of yellow jasmine drifting through the sunny woods; the warm scent of fresh plowed earth; the feebleness of newborn animals, the fluffy yellow chick balls, funny-faced calves, and long-legged colts; the mournful call of the whippoorwills; the nighttime song of peeper frogs and crickets; tiny black and gray seed and bags of fertilizer with a piercing odor that hurts your nose; hoes and rakes and plows with mules, or tractors with black exhaust fumes rising as it creeps along the furrows; the drift of pink and white blooms of peach and pear trees; the sweet tartness of dewberries with their lavender stain on the lips; lovely balmy days and stormy violent nights; sun and rain and warm earth and growing things.

The country in summer is drowsy warmth and fishing in the pond or creek; blooming flowers or plants; bearing vegetables; juicy watermelons splitting under the knife; dinners of homegrown things, meaty peas and beans, tart tomatoes, crisp cucumbers, buttery squash, and delectable onions; putting up things, field vegetables, luscious preserves of pears and peaches and figs and watermelon rind and blackberry jam and tart pickles and hot pepper sauce; the cool of empty barns with warm animal and hay smells; the satisfaction of endless rows of green growing things and the annoyance of weed and wild grass intruders; children out of school, going barefoot, making playhouses and wearing shorts or going shirtless, climbing trees and swimming all hours of the day; the busyness of full days of sun; the delicious cool of a really cool place and the tranquil watch of splendid sunset time as the deepening shadows steal their coolness over the productive earth.

The country in fall is the drifted fragrance of new-mown hay; the gathered crops, mounds of dug sweet potatoes and the last of the peas and butter beans; the rustle of dried cornstalks; the tangy freshness of turnip green and mustard and collards; the triumphant waving of blooming weed tassels, goldenrod and dandelions; the bright scarlet splash of sumac among the pines; the golden and red flames of changing leaves; muscadines hanging in deep purple clusters from the vines; the bugling of hunting dogs and the oiling of guns; the flying vees of honking geese and calling ducks winging against an evening sky; fertilizing the land, the pond, and the flower beds; raking leaves and hauling away the debris of summer; it is Halloween and Thanksgiving; treats and eats; scaring and sharing; and a covering of leaves for a tired, drained earth.

123

Black-eyed Susans in a field of early morning mist at Alexandria, New Hampshire. Photo copyright William H. Johnson, Johnson's Photography (23098-00806).

The country in winter is red berries and mistletoe and cedar Christmas trees; stark leafless branches against a gray sky; hard frost and the tracery of Jack Frost's pencil on the windows; crackling wood fires with leaping flames; nuts to roast and eat; popcorn to pop and baking to do; red noses and ears; clean cold air in the lungs; oiled tools waiting in the storehouse; filled haylofts and corn bins; Christmas presents and visits and food; snowflakes drifting down and the tracks of rabbits and field mice in the virgin snow; warm days that are harbingers of the ultimate end; stirrings deep within the earth that presage daffodils and crocus; the continuation of a recurring miracle, the earth ever renewing itself.

The country is farms, and a farm is an island of independence; a communication with the Maker; an expectation that next year, for any number of reasons, will be better. On a farm, fair or foul weather is an earthshaking problem or a sublime wish. A farm is a worked-out, worked-up piece of land ever needing replenishment. But most of all it is yours.

Thoreau gave an otherwise

hidden passion and drew from

woods and water the love

affair with earth and sky

he'd recorded in his journals.

— BERNARD MALAMUD

The log at the wood pile, the axe supported by it;
The sylvan hut, the vine over the doorway, the space cleared
for a garden,
The irregular tapping of rain down on the leaves, after the
storm is lull'd,
The wailing and moaning at intervals, the thought of the sea,
The thought of ships struck in the storm, and put on their
beam ends, and the cutting
away of masts;
The sentiment of the huge timbers of old fashion'd houses
and barns.

WALT WHITMAN

COUNTRY MEMORIES

My Prairies

I love my prairies, they are mine
From zenith to horizon line,
Clipping a world of sky and sod
Like the bended arm and wrist of God.

I love their grasses. The skies
Are larger, and my restless eyes
Fasten on more of earth and air
Than seashore furnishes anywhere.

I love the hazel thickets; and the breeze,
The never resting prairie winds. The trees
That stand like spear points high
Against the dark blue sky

Are wonderful to me. I love the gold
Of newly shaven stubble, rolled
A royal carpet toward the sun, fit to be
The pathway of a deity.

I love the life of pasture lands; the songs of birds
Are not more thrilling to me than the herd's
Mad bellowing or the shadow stride
Of mounted herdsmen at my side.

I love my prairies, they are mine
From high sun to horizon line.
The mountains and the cold gray sea
Are not for me, are not for me.

HAMLIN GARLAND

Queen Anne's Lace

The aging summer brings new grace
To dusty roadsides edged with lace
Of creamy hue and fine design
Where floral clusters intertwine.

From windswept hill it cascades down
Like blonde Chantilly on a gown;
It weaves a fragile filigree
Across the wheat field's rippling sea;

Its ivory medallions band
The grassy green of meadowland
And every obscure nook and place
Is lavish now with Queen Anne's lace.

MILLY WALTON

The Old Stone Mill

The old stone mill with the water wheel
   is still, as if it were dead,
And those who pass by on their journey to town
   think of poems and stories they've read
Of the old water mill by the turn in the bend,
   on the stream, I remember it still,
Where farmers brought wheat to grind into flour
   by the stone of the old grist mill.

It seems there's a dream from out of the past,
   an echo of long, long ago
When the old water wheel by the side of the wall
   tossed the waters to and fro.
Yet the old grist mill is tumbling away,
   though its churning it seems I still hear.
And to those who remember old-fashioned ways
   it's a memory to always hold dear.

MAXINE LYGA

The Old Barn

There is a kind of simple peace
Within this old barn door,
When muted sunlight filters through
And creeps across the floor.
Where hand-hewn beams are festooned with
The golden wisps of hay,
The spiders weave their silken threads
All through the slumberous day.

A low sweet song is drifting from
The vast dim rafter space,
Where swallows dip among the eaves
In every shadowed place.
Where setting hens are nestled deep
In quiet soft content;
The hayloft marks a season's drift
With sweet alfalfa scent.

Through all the unleashed silences
Beneath the old barn roof,
There is only but the gentle stir
Of restless, shifting hoofs.
The giant breaths of feeding stock,
A hungry calf that bawls,
Are sounds that leap with frenzied notes
Against the silent walls.

The soft tumult of song is here
Within the shadows deep,
Where the day is bright with sun and dreams
That linger in the dancing heat . . .
For there is a kind of simple peace
Within this old barn door
When moted sunlight filters through
And creeps across the floor.

JOY BELLE BURGESS

125

Spring Jottings

John Burroughs

The works of nature first acquire a meaning in the commentaries they provoke. —George Santayana

Let me say a word or two in favor of the habit of keeping a journal of one's thoughts and days. To a countryman, especially of a meditative turn, who likes to preserve the flavor of the passing moment, or to a person of leisure anywhere, who wants to make the most of life, a journal will be found a great help. It is a sort of deposit account wherein one saves up bits and fragments of his life that would otherwise be lost to him.

What seemed so insignificant in the passing, or as it lay in embryo in his mind, becomes a valuable part of his experiences when it is fully unfolded and recorded in black and white. The process of writing develops it; the bud becomes the leaf or flower; the one is disentangled from the many and takes definite form and hue. I remember that Thoreau says in a letter to a friend, after his return from a climb to the top of Monadnock, that it is not till he gets home that he really goes over the mountain; that is, I suppose, sees what the climb meant to him when he comes to write an account of it to his friend. Everyone's experience is probably much the same; when we try to tell what we saw and felt, even to our journals, we discover more and deeper meanings than we had suspected.

The pleasure and value of every walk or journey we take may be doubled to us by carefully noting down the impressions it makes upon us. How much the flavor of Maine birch I should have missed had I not compelled that vague, unconscious being within me, who absorbs so much and says so little, to unbosom himself at the point of the pen! It was not till after I got home that I really went to Maine, or to the Adirondacks, or to Canada. Out of the chaotic and nebulous impressions which these expeditions gave me, I evolved the real experience. There is hardly anything that does not become much more in the telling than in the thinking or in the feeling.

Black-eyed Susans in a field at Alexandria, New Hampshire. Photo copyright William H. Johnson, Johnson's Photography (23098-00806).

126

Lovely Beyond Expression

NATHANIEL HAWTHORNE

We stand now on the river's brink. It may well be called the Concord, the river of peace and quietness; for it is certainly the most unexcitable and sluggish stream that ever loitered imperceptibly towards its eternity—the sea. . . . Positively, I had lived three weeks beside it before it grew quite clear to my perception which way the current flowed. It never had a vivacious aspect except when a northwestern breeze is vexing its surface on a sunshiny day. From the incurable indolence of its nature, the stream is happily incapable of becoming the slave of human ingenuity, as is the fate of so many a wild, free mountain torrent. While all things else are compelled to subserve some useful purpose, it idles its sluggish life away in lazy liberty, without turning a solitary spindle or affording even water-power enough to grind the corn that grows upon its banks. . . . It slumbers between broad prairies, kissing the long meadow grass, and bathes the overhanging boughs of elder bushes and willows or the roots of elms and ash-trees and clumps of maples. . . .

In the light of a calm and golden sunset it becomes lovely beyond expression; the more lovely for the quietude that so well accords with the hour, when even the wind, after blustering all day long, usually hushes itself to rest. Each tree and rock, and every blade of grass, is distinctly imaged. . . . We will not, then, malign our river as gross and impure while it can glorify itself with so adequate a picture of the heaven that broods over it; or, if we remember its tawny blue and the muddiness of its bed, let it be a symbol that the earthliest human soul has an infinite spiritual capacity and may contain the better world within its depths.

129

Joe-Pye-weed along Indian Stream, Pittsburg, New Hampshire. Photo copyright William H. Johnson, Johnson's Photography (53075-00102).

Chapter Seven

SCENES
AND
SEASONS

Spring

GLADYS TABER

*Sweet spring, full of sweet days
and roses, A box where sweets
compacted lie.* —GEORGE HERBERT

April in New England is like first love. There is the tender excitement of gathering the first snowdrops, the only symbol of life in the deserted garden. They are the lyric expression of music to come—as the symphony of lilacs will surely come—because I am picking the cool delicate bells of this first flower. When I brought the first tiny bouquet in and put it in an antique pill bottle, the greenish glass was the color of the center of the snowdrops. I often wonder what pills went in the bottles for they are only half an inch to an inch high and pencil-slim. My own pill bottles look gigantic in comparison! And when I swallow my vitamins, I feel as if I were choking down acorns. . . .

But like first love, April has bitter days. This morning, we woke to a sky as dark as the inside of a snow boot. Leftover wind from March crashed branches to the ground that had withstood all of the winter blizzards. The pond iced over in the night again, and as I made pancakes for breakfast, I had a silly fancy that winter had flung her last scarf across it because she did not need it any longer. The confused robins tipped around in a wormless world, and the winter birds made almost as much noise as a social hour after a Woman's Club meeting. The red-winged blackbirds swooped down from the sugar maples, and it seemed to me they sounded cross.

I could imagine the wives saying crossly to their mates that it was all their fault they had come north too soon. So I went out after breakfast to set up the birds' buffet. For a time we shall have both the winter birds that companioned us during the long cold, and the migratory ones coming from strange southern lands. The air is filled with the excitement of wings. However, much as I welcome the wanderers, I love most the chickadees, nuthatches, and woodpeckers, for they have shared the bitter season with us, and never a blizzard too fierce for them to chatter away at the window feeder. I suspect we always love best those who share the hard things with us. Spring and summer friends are delightful, but give me winter friends for my dearest.

As I went back to the house to turn up the thermostat, I reflected that Stillmeadow has seen a lot of sharing since it was built in 1690. In the beginning, it was a world in itself,

THE IDEALS COUNTRY TREASURY

for the village was a long way off when you had to walk there or hitch up the horse. (It takes about five minutes now.) Families, in the early days, were units. They had to be. Aside from flour, molasses, tea, and salt, most of the food was grown on the farm. Hams were smoked in the small smokehouse, home-grown herbs went into spicy sausage and scrapple at butchering time. Lye and wood ashes cooked in the big iron kettle we now use for kindling. I always imagine it still smells of soft soap. The carder and spinning wheel were busy. Fuel for the great fireplace and the three lesser fireplaces came from the wood lot up the hill, and all the cooking was done over the fire. Savory stews bubbled in the iron pot hanging over the embers, potatoes baked in the ashes, "punkin" pies went in the Dutch oven and came forth spicy and rich, and made a fine end to a supper eaten by firelight and the glow from tallow dips.

The end of winter in those days was a miracle, even more than now. For in April the heated warmers for the beds upstairs could be discarded. The featherbeds were warm enough. And the three-hour sermon in the unheated church was more comfortable when you no longer wrapped hot bricks or stones or flatirons and held them in your lap.

In April, then, as now, the men of the house went up to the wood lot to cut for next season. A countryman's life always moves steadily, with a pattern fitting the changing season. This week our neighbor, Joe, said he better get up to the wood lot. He does not have to chop and haul by hand. He has a small trailer to load the wood on, and he has a modern saw. But the pattern itself is the same. When the snow melt leaves a way to the woods open, the wood is cut.

The logs come down the hill to be piled near the back door against the next winter. The true country dweller is a conservationist, and always cuts to keep the woods in good shape. In New England, we cut with an eye to taking out dying trees, lightning-blasted ones, or fallen old apple trees. Clearing out the dead apple trees, for instance, makes room for the new shoots which spring up around the old trunk. So another generation, God willing, will have a young orchard of wild apple trees on which, if they are so minded, they can graft any number of fancy apples.

Wood is still our staple for heat. A good many of our neighbors burn wood in their furnaces. Those who have gone so modern as to install coal or oil-burning units, still have the problem of four or five fireplaces in the pre-Revolutionary houses. I have yet to know of a central heating system that will prevent winter from walking right down a chimney, and indeed, in our house, it snows on the hearth unless we have a fire.

When we turn the thermostat up, it is hot as a freshly boiled egg in the kitchen, but the family room is still as cold as a polar bear. So when April walks over the countryside, we all hope we still have enough wood in the woodpile for a fire in the fireplace on cool summer evenings.

As the long lovely light of April falls on the meadow lately deep in snow, I think about the way time passes. "Time is but the stream I go fishing in," said Thoreau. "I drink at it; but while I drink, I see the sandy bottom and detect how shallow it is. Its thin current slides away, but eternity remains." I am not sure I understand this, for I am no philosopher, but it stretches my mind. The days I live now in the beginning of spring are certainly transient, dusk falls before I have sufficiently enjoyed the dew on the grass in early morning. We busy ourselves with all the things that must, we think, be done at once. "But eternity remains," said Thoreau. Days on the calendar come and go, but God is timeless. Love and faith and hope know no season, they are themselves, I think, eternity.

And, in a sense, the miracle of spring is eternal also.

"Let us spend one day as deliberately as Nature," said Thoreau. Nature never hurries, season moves gently into season, day into night.

If we would all, now and then, spend one day as deliberately as nature, we would have less tensions, less anxieties. We would find, I am sure, reserves of peace in ourselves.

And be renewed, as spring renews the frozen earth.

A spring snow is somehow unconvincing. The old wellhouse has an extra peaked roof of pearl. The yard is drifted. The branches of the lilacs are outlined in silver and have a Japanese look. But even as we shovel out to the gate, we take a casual attitude. For it is spring, and snow cannot last. The Farmer's Almanac says "Nothing wrong here, except the last big snow of the year." The Almanac is a faithful friend and more often right than wrong. And the neighbor down the road says the peepers have to be frozen in three times, and I should not worry about them. This is only twice.

At the end of April we hope it will be dry enough to plough. In late springs, ploughing may come so late as to be almost a disaster. The ground must be dry, and friable, so the earth can be picked up in handfuls and not be sticky. Farmers go out and pick up a bit of dirt and crumble it and watch it fall back to the ground, and then they know. Ploughing is a testament to life, as planting is a testament to growth. . . . Ploughing, planting, hoeing, harvesting, have been the way of life here for well over two hundred years, and no matter what goes on in the world, we follow the swing of the seasons as we always have.

When that special morning comes and I hear the plough, I run out to wave at the neighbor who says he "will turn her over, and then harrow." The great blades of the plough flash, the freed earth rises in dark waves. Boulders come up too. The ploughing leaves deep furrows and great chunks of dirt, so the garden looks like a small, but rough sea. After it is sunned a day or so, the harrow goes over and levels it off. Then Jill rakes the small stones out,

marks the rows with string tied to stakes at each end of the garden. The seed packages are opened, and now we are on the way again. It's a good time.

Tamping the earth down firmly, Jill says, "Now we need a soaking rain." Sometimes we get it, but if we don't, she lugs pails of water from the pond to encourage the seeds to sprout. If it rains too much, seeds can rot in the ground, in which case you simply replant and hope for the best.

Down by the pond, the dogtooth violets are pale gold. Who planted them in the beginning? Nature herself, I reflect, is the best planter of all. The cockers and Irish race about, popping young frogs off the bank. Fish are beginning to jump at dusk as the water warms.

There is a great sense of life stirring in the swamp above the pond, and the upper hills are frosted with green. As the dogs fly up to the brook which feeds the pond, I wonder about the dogs the Indians had, for the Indians obviously had a camp at this spot. We were so told by an expert, but also told by all the signs we have found during the past. The stream would have been wider then, and the spot sheltered and safe. Maize would grow where our corn now stands. Fish were plentiful. There was plenty of firewood, for the woods were thick, and still are, for that matter.

As planting time comes around, there is excitement in the air. The main planting comes in May, when the maples are in leaf, but lettuce and radishes and snow peas go in as soon as the ground is workable. It took us some years to learn, however, that you cannot go against the rhythm of Nature. We wasted a mort of seeds getting our whole garden in when the ground was as cold as a gangster's heart. In the damp chilly earth, the seeds simply sat. Finally we learned to wait until the ground was dry, warm, and friable. Later plantings caught up with the earlier ones and went on to bear well.

What soil we have in Connecticut in the valley is good soil, rich enough, and not heavy. The trouble is, there is not enough of it. Rocks and boulders take up most of the space, and no matter how carefully you clear the land, another winter brings up a whole new crop, bigger and better. No Midwest farmer would bother with our land at all, but the true New Englander gets a lot of good out of those stones. The miles of grey stone fences that mark the fields and roadsides were all built when somebody was clearing the land. The stone foundations for barns and the old houses came right to hand from the cornfield. Our own fourteen-foot square chimney and the hand-hewn blocks of silvery stone for the fireplaces must have come from our own garden, for it is evident that the first owner of the house planted his carrots and potatoes and squash right where we do. He couldn't help it, for great ledges and the swamp wouldn't have made a garden.

The rich, black soil of the Midwest, and the dark rosy red soil of Virginia are beautiful. But there is a sense of achievement when you finally get a crowbar under a maddeningly solid boulder and move it up an inch! And the small stones that we gather are cool and polished, and shot with color. Possibly my love for stones comes from Father's being a geologist, so that I grew up with the feeling that a stone was exciting. . . .

Spring has a special smell. As the sun dries the tree trunks and branches, bark gives off a clean odor. The pines add spicy fragrance to the air. Then there is the musty smell of leaves as we rake the yard, for no matter how carefully we rake in autumn, spring always finds leftover windrows under the sugar maples and apple trees. The earth itself has a damp sweetness. And it may be my imagination, but the snow-fed water of the pond has a fresh cool odor.

Foal with its mother in dandelion-covered pasture near Morton, Washington. Photo copyright Steve Terrill (WA-6-6-106).

135

A Walk in the Spring

MICHAEL FAIRLESS

March violets bloomed under the sheltered hedge with here and there a pale primrose; a frosted bramble spray still held its autumn tints clinging to the semblance of the past; and great branches of snowy blackthorn broke the barren hedgeway as if spring made a mock of winter's snows.

Light of heart and foot with the new wine of the year, I sped on again, stray daffodils lighting the wayside, until I heard the voice of the stream, and reached the field gate which leads to the lower meadows. There before me lay spring's pageant; green pennons waving, dainty maids curtsying, and a host of joyous yellow trumpeters proclaiming "Victory" to an awakened earth.

At the upper end of the field, the river provides yet closer sanctuary for these children of the spring. Held in its embracing arms lies an island long and narrow, some thirty-feet-by-twelve, a veritable untrod Eldorado, glorious in gold from end to end, a fringe of reeds by the water's edge and daffodils. I sat down . . . blue sky overhead, green grass at my feet decked in glorious sheen; a sea of triumphant, golden heads tossing blithely back as the wind swept down to play with them at his pleasure.

It was all mine to have and to hold without severing a single slender stem or harboring a thought of covetousness; mine, as the whole earth was mine, to appropriate to myself without the burden and bane of worldly possession.

The Yellow Violet

Oft, in the sunless April day,
    Thy early smile has stayed my walk;
But midst the gorgeous blooms of May,
    I passed thee on thy humble stalk.

So they, who climb to wealth, forget
    The friends in darker fortunes tried.

I copied them—but I regret
    That I should ape the ways of pride.

And when again the genial hour
    Awakes the painted tribes of light,
I'll not o'er look the modest flower
    That made the woods of April bright.

WILLIAM CULLEN BRYANT

Blue violet and grasses after a spring rain in White Mountain National Forest in Woodstock, New Hampshire. Photo copyright William H. Johnson, Johnson's Photography (23098-00912).

Rain

How beautiful is the rain!
After the dust and heat,
In the broad and fiery street,
In the narrow lane,
How beautiful is the rain!

How it clatters along the roofs,
Like the tramp of hoofs!
How it gushes and struggles out
From the throat of the overflowing spout
Across the window-pane
It pours and pours;
And swift and wide,
With a muddy tide,
Like a river down the gutter roars
The rain, the welcome rain!

From the neighboring school
Come the boys,
With more than their wonted noise
And commotion;

And down the wet streets
Sail their mimic fleets,
Till the treacherous pool
Ingulfs them in its whirling
And turbulent ocean.

In the country, on every side,
Where far and wide,
Like a leopard's tawny and spotted hide,
Stretches the plain,
To the dry grass and the drier grain
How welcome is the rain!

Near at hand,
The farmer sees
His pastures, and his fields of grain,
As they bend their tops
To the numberless beating drops
Of the incessant rain.
He counts it as no sin
That he sees therein
Only his own thrift and gain.

HENRY WADSWORTH LONGFELLOW

THE GROWING SEASONS

Sing a song of seasons!
Something bright in all!
Flowers in the Summer,
Fires in the Fall.

ROBERT LOUIS STEVENSON

Beneath the crisp and wintry carpet hid
A million buds but stay their blossoming;
And trustful birds have built their nests amid
The shuddering boughs, and only wait to sing
Till one soft shower from the south shall bid,
And hither tempt the pilgrim steps of Spring.

ROBERT BRIDGES

My Heart Leaps Up

My heart leaps up when I behold
    A rainbow in the sky:
So was it when my life began;
So it is now I am a man;
So be it when I shall grow old,
    Or let me die!
The Child is father of the Man;
And I could wish my days to be
Bound each to each with natural piety.

WILLIAM WORDSWORTH

Early Spring

Once more the Heavenly Power
    Makes all things new,
And domes the red-plow'd hills
    With loving blue;
The blackbirds have their wills,
    The thistles too.

Opens a door in heaven;
    From skies of glass
A Jacob's ladder falls
    On greening grass,
And o'er the mountain-walls
    Young angels pass.

For now the Heavenly Power
    Makes all things new,
And thaws the cold, and fills
    The flower with dew;
The blackbirds have their wills,
    The poets too.

ALFRED, LORD TENNYSON

The High-Tide of the Year

Now is the high-tide of the year,
And whatever of life hath ebbed away
Comes flooding back with a ripply cheer,
Into every bare inlet and creek and bay;
Now the heart is so full that a drop overfills it,
We are happy now because God wills it;
No matter how barren the past may have been,
Tis enough for us now that the leaves are green;
We sit in the warm shade and feel right well
How the sap creeps up and the blossoms swell.

We may shut our eyes, but we cannot help knowing
That skies are clear and grass is growing;
The breeze comes whispering in our ear,
That dandelions are blossoming near,
That maize has sprouted, that streams are flowing,
That the river is bluer than the sky,
That the robin is plastering his house nearby;
And if the breeze kept the good news back,
For other couriers we should not lack;
We could guess it all by yon heifer's lowing,
And hark! how clear bold Chanticleer,
Warmed with the new wine of the year,
Tells all in his lusty crowing!

JAMES RUSSELL LOWELL

To sit in the shade on a fine day and look upon verdure is the most perfect refreshment. —JANE AUSTEN

Warm Days

Henry David Thoreau

I only know that summer sang in me . . .

—Edna St. Vincent Millay

I yearn for those old, meandering, dry, uninhabited roads which lead away from town, which lead us away from temptation, which conduct to the outside of earth, over its uppermost crust; where you may forget in what country you are travelling, where no farmer can complain that you are treading down his grass, no gentleman who has recently constructed a seat in the country that you are trespassing; on which you can go off at half cock and wave adieu to the village; along which you may travel like a pilgrim, going towhiter. Where travellers are not too often to be met; where my spirit is free; where the walls and the fences are not cared for; where your head is more in heaven than your feet on earth; which have long reaches where you can see the approaching traveller half a mile off and be prepared for him; not so luxuriant a soil as to attract men; some root and stump fences which do not need attention; where travellers have no occasion to stop, but pass along and leave you to your thoughts. Where it makes no odds which way you face, whether you are going or coming, whether it is morning or evening, midnoon or midnight; where earth is cheap enough by being public; where you can walk and think with least obstruction, there being nothing to measure progress by. Where you can pace when your breast is full, and cherish your moodiness; where you are not false in relations with men, are not dining nor conversing with them; by which you may go to the uttermost parts of the earth. It is wide enough, wide as the thoughts it allows to visit you.

What more luxuriant than a clover field. The poorest soil that is covered with it looks incomparably fertile. This is perhaps the most characteristic feature of June, resounding with the hum of insects, such a blush on the fields. The rude health of the sorrel cheek has given place to the blush of clover. Painters are wont, in their pictures of Paradise, to strew the field too thickly with flowers. There should be moderation in all things. Though we love flowers we do not want them so thick under our feet that we cannot walk without treading on them. But a clover field in bloom is some excuse for them.

How satisfactory is the fragrance of this flower! It is the

emblem of purity. It reminds me of a young country maiden. It is just so simple and unproved. Wholesome as the odor of the cow. It is not a highly refined odor, but merely a fresh youthful morning sweetness. It is merely the unalloyed sweetness of the earth and the water; a fair opportunity and field for life; like its petals, uncolored by any experience; a simple maiden on her way to school, her face surrounded by a white ruff. But how quickly it becomes the prey of insects!

As I was going up the hill, I was surprised to see rising above the June grass, near a walnut, a whitish object, like a stone with a white top, or a skunk erect, for it was black below. It was an enormous toadstool, or fungus, a sharply conical parasol in the form of a sugar loaf, slightly turned up at the edges, which were rent half an inch for every inch or two. It was so delicate and fragile that its whole cap trembled at the least touch, and as I could not lay it down without injuring it, I was obliged to carry it home all the way in my hand, erect, while I paddled my boat with one hand. It was a wonder how its soft cone ever broke through the earth.

This is the most glorious part of this day, the serenest, warmest, brightest part, and the most suggestive. Evening is fairer than morning. It is a chaste eve, for it has sustained the trials of the day, but to the morning such praise was inapplicable. It is incense-breathing. Morning is full of promise and vigor. Evening is pensive. I enjoy now the warmth of summer with some of the prospect of spring.

Golden mountain arnicas along Big Creek in Medicine Bow National Forest in Carbon County, Wyoming. Photo copyright Steve Terrill (WY-13-7-26).

HEARTH AND HOME

Wheat

HAMLIN GARLAND

As I look back over my life on that Iowa farm, the song of the reaper fills a large place in my mind. We were all worshippers of wheat in those days. The men thought and talked of little else between seeding and harvest, and you will not wonder at this if you have known and bowed before such abundance as we then enjoyed. Deep as the breast of a man, wide as the sea, heavy-headed, supple-stocked, many-voiced, full of multitudinous, secret, whispered colloquies—a meeting place of winds and of sunlight—our fields ran to the world's end.

We trembled when the storm lay hard upon the wheat, we exulted as the lilac shadows of noonday drifted over it! We went out into it at noon when all was still—so still we could hear the pulse of the transforming sap as it crept from cool root to swaying plume. We stood before it at evening when the setting sun flooded it with crimson, the bearded heads lazily swirling under the wings of the wind, the mousing hawk dipping into its green deeps like the eagle into the sea, and our hearts expanded with the beauty and the mystery of it—and back of all this was the knowledge that its abundance meant a new carriage, an addition to the house, or a new suit of clothes.

Haying was over, and day by day we boys watched with deepening interest while the hot sun transformed the juices of the soil into those stately stalks. I loved to go out into the fairy forest of it, and lying there, silent in its swaying deeps, hear the wild chickens peep and the wind sing its subtle song over our heads.

143

A wheat field on an August morning near Montana. Photo copyright Jeff Gnass (25-1955-401).

In Swimming-Time

James Whitcomb Riley

Clouds above, as white as wool, drifting over skies as blue as the eyes of beautiful children when they smile at you: groves of maple, elm, and beech, with the sunshine sifted through branches, mingling each with each, dim with shade and bright with dew. Stripling trees and poplars hoar, hickory and sycamore, and the drowsy dogwood bowed where the ripples laugh aloud, and the crooning creek is stirred to a gaiety that now mates the warble of the bird teetering on the hazel-bough. Grasses long and fine and fair as your schoolboy-sweetheart's hair, backward roached and twirled and twined by the fingers of the wind.

Vines and mosses, interlinked down dark aisles and deep ravines, where the stream runs, willow-brinked, round a bend where some one leans faint and vague and indistinct as the like-reflected thing in the current shimmering. Childish voices further on, where the truant stream has gone, vex the echoes of the wood till no word is understood—save that one is well aware happiness is hiding there. There, in leafy coverts, little bodies poise and leap, spattering the solitude and the silence everywhere—mimic monsters of the deep!

Wallowing the sandy shoals—plunging headlong out of sight; and, with spurtings of delight, clutching hands, and slippery soles, climbing up the treacherous steep over which the spring-board spurns each again as he returns. Purple lips and chattering teeth, eyes that burn, but, in beneath, every care beyond recall, every task forgotten quite, and again, in dreams at night, dropping, drifting through it all!

The Fisherman

Along a stream that raced and ran
  Through tangled trees and over stones,
That long had heard the pipes o' Pan
  And shared the joys that nature owns,
I met a fellow fisherman,
  Who greeted me in cheerful tones.

"Out here," he told me, with a smile,
  "Away from all the city's sham,
The strife for splendor and for style,
the ticker and the telegram
I come for just a little while
  To be exactly as I am."

Foes think the bad in him they've guessed
  And prate about the wrong they scan;
Friends that have seen him at his best
  Believe they know his every plan;
I know him better than the rest,
  I know him as a fisherman.

Edgar A. Guest

Boat and dock with autumn reflection in Little Birch Lake in Laona, Wisconsin. Photo copyright Darryl Beers (MT-10Y49-52).

Exactly What, Why, and When Is Indian Summer?

JUDSON HALE, SR.

No spring, nor summer beauty hath such grace, As I have seen in one autumnal face. —JOHN DONNE

After Labor Day has passed, it seems that almost any warm day in the northern part of the United States is referred to by most people as "Indian summer." And while their mistake is certainly not of the earthshaking variety, these casual observers are, for the most part, in error.

Besides falling within specific dates, true Indian summer must meet certain other criteria. It must be warm, of course. In addition, however, the atmosphere must be hazy or smoky, there must be no wind, the barometer must be standing high, and the nights must be clear and chilly.

The more controversial aspect of Indian summer is the time of its occurrence—or whether there is a certain time. Most would agree that warm days in the fall do not of themselves constitute Indian summer unless they follow a spell of cold weather or a hard frost. Beyond that, many references to Indian summer in American literature indicate that it occurs in late fall.

For the past two hundred years, this publication, as well as many other nineteenth-century almanacs, has adhered to the saying, "If All Saints' brings out winter, St. Martin's brings out Indian summer." Accordingly, Indian summer can occur between St. Martin's Day (November 11) and November 20. If the conditions that constitute Indian summer do not occur between those dates, then there is no Indian summer that year. If a period of warm fall weather occurs at a different time, such a period could be correctly described as being like Indian summer.

Finally, why is Indian summer called Indian summer? Some say the name comes from the Indians, who believed that the condition was caused by a certain wind emanating from the court of their god, Cautantowwit, or the southwestern god. Oth-

146

ers say that the term evolved from the fact that the deciduous trees around the time of Indian summer are "dressed" as colorfully as Indians.

The most probable origin of the name, in our view, goes back to the very early settlers in New England. Each year they would welcome the arrival of cold wintry weather in late October, knowing that they could leave their stockades without worrying about Indian attacks and could begin preparing their fields for spring planting. The Indians didn't like attacking in cold weather. But then came a time, almost every year around St. Martin's Day, when it would suddenly turn warm again, and the Indians would decide to have one more go at the settlers. The settlers called this Indian summer.

Frost covers red maples and grasses in a swamp in Piscataquis County, Maine. Photo copyright William H. Johnson, Johnson's Photography (52094-00104).

These Are the Days

These are the days when birds come back—
A very few—a Bird or two—
To take a backward look. . . .

Oh, fraud that cannot cheat the bee—
Almost thy plausibility
Induces my belief,

Till ranks of seeds their witness bear—
And softly thro' the altered air
Hurries a timid leaf.

Oh sacrament of summer days,
Oh, Last Communion in the Haze—
Permit a child to join,

Thy sacred emblems to partake—
Thy consecrated bread to take,
Taste thin immortal wine!

EMILY DICKINSON

147

Thy bounty shines in autumn unconfined, And spreads a common feast for all that lives. —JAMES THOMSON

O it sets my heart a clickin'
Like the tickin' of a clock,
When the frost is on the punkin
And the fodder's in the shock.

JAMES WHITCOMB RILEY

*Behold congenial Autumn comes,
The Sabbath of the year!* —JOHN LOGAN

Autumn Flowers

Those few pale autumn flowers,
How beautiful they are!
Than all that went before,
Than all the summer's store,
How lovelier by far!

And why? They are the last—
The last!—the last!—the last—
Oh, by that little word,
How many thoughts are stirred!
That whisper of the past!

Pale flowers!—pale, perishing flowers!
You're types of precious things,
Types of those bitter moments
That flit, like life's enjoyments,
On rapid, rapid wings.

CAROLINE ANNE SOUTHEY

148

AUTUMN'S GLORY

The Corn Song

Heap high the farmer's wintry hoard!
Heap high the golden corn!
No richer gift has Autumn poured
From out her lavish horn!

We dropped the seed o'er hill and plain
Beneath the sun of May,
And frightened from our sprouting grain
The robber crows away.

All through the long bright days of June
Its leaves grew green and fair,
And waved in hot midsummer's noon
Its soft and yellow hair.

And now, with Autumn's moonlit eyes,
Its harvesttime has come,
We pluck away the frosted leaves,
And bear the treasure home.

JOHN GREENLEAF WHITTIER

September

The golden-rod is yellow;
    The corn is turning brown;
The trees in apple orchards
    With fruit are bending down.

The gentian's bluest fringes
    Are curling in the sun;
In dusty pods the milkweed
    Its hidden silk has spun.

The sedges flaunt their harvest,
    In every meadow nook;
And asters by the brook-side
    Make asters in the brook,

From dewy lanes at morning
    The grapes; sweet odors rise;
At noon the roads all flutter
    With yellow butterflies.

By all these lovely tokens
    September days are here,
With summer's best of weather,
    And autumn's best of cheer.

But none of all this beauty
    Which floods the earth and air
Is unto me the secret
    Which makes September fair.

'Tis a thing which I remember;
    To name it thrills me yet:
One day so on September
    I never can forget.

HELEN HUNT JACKSON

The Rapture of the Year

While skies glint bright with bluest light
Through clouds that race o'er field and town,
And leaves go dancing left and right,
And orchard apples tumble down;
While schoolgirls sweet, in lane or street,
Lean against the wind and feel and hear
Its glad heart like a lover's beat—
So reigns the rapture of the year.

Then ho! and hey! and whoop-hooray!
Though winter clouds be looming,
Remember a November day
Is merrier than mildest May
With all her blossoms blooming.

While birds in scattered flight are blown
Aloft and lost in dusky mist,
And truant boys scud home alone
Neath skies of gold and amethyst;
While twilight falls, and echo calls
Across the haunted atmosphere,
With low, sweet laughs at intervals,
So reigns the rapture of the year

Then ho! and hey! and whoop-hooray!
Though winter clouds be looming,
Remember a November day
Is merrier than mildest May
With all her blossoms blooming.

JAMES WHITCOMB RILEY

Earth sitteth still, and is

at rest. —ZECHARIAH 1:11

Thoughts on Autumn

NATHANIEL HAWTHORNE

Still later in the season Nature's tenderness waxes stronger. It is impossible not to be fond of our mother now; for she is so fond of us! At other periods she does not make this impression on me, or only at rare intervals; but in these genial days of autumn, when she has perfected her harvests and accomplished every needful thing that was given her to do, then she overflows with a blessed superfluity of love. She has leisure to caress her children now. It is good to be alive at such times.

Thank Heaven for breath—yes, for mere breath—when it is made up of a heavenly breeze like this! It comes with a real kiss upon our cheeks; it would linger fondly around us if it might; but since it must be gone, it embraces us with its whole kindly heart and passes onward to embrace likewise the next thing that it meets. A blessing is flung abroad and scattered far and wide over the earth, to be gathered up by all who choose.

I recline upon the still unwithered grass and whisper to myself, "O perfect day! O beautiful world! O beneficent God!" And it is the promise of a blessed eternity; for our Creator would never have made such lovely days and have given us the deep hearts to enjoy them, above and beyond all thought, unless we were meant to be immortal. This sunshine is the golden pledge thereof. It beams through the gates of paradise and shows us glimpses far inward.

150

An autumn colored cherry orchard at the Columbia River Gorge National Scenic Area near Mosier, Oregon. Photo copyright Steve Terrill (OR-13-11-414).

Country Chronicle

LANSING CHRISTMAN

Walk in the soft September fields and listen to the sermons from the hills. God will speak to you through nature. There will be psalms in woodland and meadow, scriptures and songs in pasture and babbling brook. Now at summer's end, it is as if the creation of the world has been completed, and nature in its sabbath sings hosannas on high.

Walk in the September fields, and they will hold out their arms and embrace you, friend to friend. The rush of the growing season is behind us. In this early autumn sun, sense the warmth and rhythm of life. Rest for a while on a lichened stone and tune your inner being to the glory of nature. The glory of early fall is that of accomplishment and satisfaction. Each golden September field wears the gentle glow of the mother who has seen her young fly on from the nest and become a part of this great world. Each combed September field shows the polished serenity of hard work rewarded. The colors of September are the colors of glory.

Leaves of the hickories shine in their golden hues, and the reds of woodbine climb fence and tree. The earth is warmed by the scarlet of soft maples and sumac and the first feathery lemon-colored blooms of witch hazel on the ledge. The purples of the aster and the blazing flames of the goldenrod defy the hint of winter in the chilling evening breeze.

The fields are friendly and kind, and music can be heard from thicket and tree, from grass, and from running water near the glade. The meadowlark whistles as it takes flight from its fence-post perch. The air is pierced by the sharp chrring of the woodchuck near its burrow on the farm's sidehill where it has been feeding on clover, preparing for its winter of sleep. Listen to the chipmunks and crickets, the bluebird's warble from an aging apple tree, the sweet refrain of the song sparrow from the alders down by the marsh.

Year-round, I go to the fields and listen. And God speaks to me through the wonder of His Creation. The fields befriend me anew each time I go to them for deep meditation. Yes, I am forever a friend to the fields.

153

Goldenrod and purple loosestrife growing in Button Bay State Park, Vermont. Photo copyright William H. Johnson, Johnson's Photography (54698-00105).

Ice Harvest

R. J. McGinnis

And Winter slumbering in the open air, Wears on his smiling face a dream of Spring! — AUTHOR UNKNOWN

Icehouses, once common enough on the better farms of America, have, with few exceptions, long ago been made over into extra chicken houses or split up into kindling wood. The decline set in about fifty years ago when mechanical refrigeration and power lines began to go to the country. There are a few survivors, some in isolated parts of New England where the high lines have not yet penetrated, some at the less fancy summer resorts.

To put up ice one must have good water—a pond or lake, a river or stream with a sizable pool of deep water. Many of the first farm ponds were built, not to supply water but to supply ice.

The ice harvest usually came toward the end of January or early in February, when the ice was about ten-inches thick. The best temperature for cutting was a few degrees below freezing, so the water would freeze quickly on the cakes after they were taken out of the pond. But it seemed that it never was a pleasant twenty-five degrees; frequently it was zero or below. Men did not dare to wait, far too often a zero spell in the Northern states is followed by a thaw which would spoil the ice.

After the snow was scraped from an area, the ice was "plowed out." The ice plow was a weighted, horse-drawn contrivance with a row of sharp teeth which cut a narrow furrow six or seven inches deep. A marker scratched a line for the next cut. The plow was run one way over an area, then over the other at right angles, plowing out a checkerboard pattern of cakes of a more or less standard size, twenty-two inches by twelve inches, weighing about a hundred pounds. Sometimes the cakes were broken apart with a bar, but particular people liked to have the edges smooth, so the last two or three inches were sawed by hand. The ice saw was straight-bladed and four or five feet in length with a handle like a lawn mower.

After the cakes were cut, they were poled through the dark water to the shore. Here a long plank sloped into the water; the trick was to give the cake of ice enough momentum so that its weight would carry it up where someone with a pair of tongs could snag it. Every year, it seemed, someone fell in; he either lost his footing or his pole skidded. The lad was fished out, rushed to the nearest house, and hustled into the kitchen to warm by a crackling fire in the big range. He was peeled to his birthday suit, rubbed down, and then got into dry clothes. This was followed by two or three cups of strong coffee and a few doughnuts, a treatment pleasant enough to make a lad consider falling in purposely.

Half a century ago the ice was hauled to the icehouse on two-horse bobsleds. Layer by layer the old weathered icehouse was filled. A sprinkling of dry sawdust was scattered between each layer of cakes. This made them easier to separate when they were taken out. A two-foot-wide layer of sawdust was tamped lightly between the ice and sides of the building. After the last layer was pushed up the long, oak plank, the whole heap was covered a yard deep with sawdust.

Some farmers not only cut ice for their own needs, but supplied it for neighbors. The going price was five cents a cake. But the thrifty farmers owned their own ice-cutting equipment. It took an average of three hundred cakes to last a family through the summer; at five cents a cake this was fifteen dollars, one-third the price of a good cow.

Time was when ice harvesting was a major industry in the northern half of the United States. No one knows when a farsighted colonial farmer first conceived the idea of storing ice to use in hot weather. Old records reveal that many icehouses were built in New England after the Revolution. An entry in George Washington's diary shows that he stored ice in winter. The diary, dated 1785, says "Having put the heavy frame into my Ice House, I began this day to seal it with Boards."

As towns grew into cities in the first half of the nineteenth century, the demand for ice grew rapidly. Within a few miles of the major population centers, gigantic rough-board icehouses were built on the shores of ponds, lakes, and rivers. Ice for New York City was cut and stored 150 miles up the Hudson; every day the loaded ice barges went to the city.

Ice became a spectacular item of international commerce. In 1805, Frederick Tudor of Boston conceived the idea of sending ice by ships to the West Indies where ice had never been seen. In the next thirty years, Tudor made a fortune shipping the cold luxury to the West and the East Indies, to South America, China, and England. In 1853, A. J. Downing, one of America's famous pioneer landscape architects, wrote, "American ice has sent into positive ecstasies all those of the great metropolis (London) who depend upon their throats for sensations."

One of the most important centers of ice cutting was the Kennebec River in Maine. Thousands of men and youths gathered to work for the big companies; farmers came down from upper Maine, up from Massachusetts, and east from New Hampshire. The companies built stove-heated barracks to house the workers' barracks as barren as the giant storage houses for the ice. Some of the ice houses were six hundred feet long with double-boarded walls, insulated with sawdust between the walls.

As the cakes shot up the chutes, powered by gasoline engines, they were forced through planers which cut all cakes to uniform depth and width. And when spring came and the river ice went out, a fleet of schooners came and loaded the ice cakes. Then the ships scattered for the places of earth with their valuable cargoes.

Each year the ice harvest grows smaller. A farmer no longer has to freeze himself in winter to keep cool in summer.

Winter

RALPH WALDO EMERSON

$\mathcal{I}$ see the spectacle of morning from the hilltop over against my house, from daybreak to sunrise, with emotions which an angel might share. The long slender bars of cloud float like fishes in the sea of crimson light. From the earth, as a shore, I look out into that silent sea. I seem to partake of its rapid transformations; the active enchantment reaches my dust, and I dilate and conspire with the morning wind. How does Nature defy us with a few and cheap elements! Give me health and a day, and I will make the pomp of emperors ridiculous. The dawn is my Assyria; the sunset and moonrise my Paphos. . . .

Not less excellent, except for our less susceptibility in the afternoon, was the charm, last evening of a January sunset. The western clouds divided and subdivided themselves into pink flakes modulated with tints of unspeakable softness, and the air had so much life and sweetness that it was a pain to come within doors. . . . The leafless trees became spires of flame in the sunset, with the blue east for their background, and the stars of the dead chalices of flowers, and every withered stem and stubble rimed with frost, contribute something to the mute music.

Winter's Fruit

HENRY DAVID THOREAU

$\mathcal{T}$ he snow hangs on the trees as the fruit of the season. In those twigs which the winter has preserved naked there is a warmer green for the contrast. The whole tree exhibits a kind of interior and household comfort, a sheltered and covert aspect. It has the snug inviting look of a cottage on the moors, buried in snow. Our voices ring hollowly through the woods as through a chamber; the twigs crackle underfoot with private and household echoes. I have observed on a clear winter's morning that the woods have their southern window as well as the house, through which the first beams of the sun stream along their aisles and corridors. The sun goes up swiftly behind the limbs of the white pine, as the sashes of a window.

The Pemigewasset River and Falls after winter's first snowfall in the Franconia Notch State Park, New Hampshire. Photo copyright William H. Johnson, Johnson's Photography (23070-00812).

HEARTH AND HOME

Index

Italics indicate photograph • Caps Indicate Titles of Chapters and Special Spreads

The Ideals Country Treasury

160